NAPOLEON III—MAN OF DESTINY

EUROPEAN PROBLEM STUDIES

Under the editorial direction of
HENRY BERTRAM HILL

The Fall of Rome—MORTIMER CHAMBERS

The Renaissance Debate—DENYS HAY

Napoleon III—Man of Destiny—BRISON D. GOOCH

The Unification of Italy—CHARLES F. DELZELL

British Imperialism—ROBIN W. WINKS

Hitler and Nazi Germany—ROBERT G. L. WAITE

NAPOLEON III–
MAN OF DESTINY

Enlightened Statesman or Proto-Fascist?

Edited by BRISON D. GOOCH
University of Oklahoma

HOLT, RINEHART AND WINSTON
New York • Chicago • San Francisco • Toronto • London

CONTENTS

INTRODUCTION

In December 1852 Louis Napoleon took the title of Napoleon III. The "consular" transition from republic to empire had lasted only a year. In the next eighteen years he ruled over a France which was enjoying an amazing period of industrial growth. Dramatic successes in foreign policy were achieved by the emperor in the early, authoritarian phase of his rule, while later, as he was progressively liberalizing his regime, failures came in rapid succession.

The Second Empire stands as a lengthy episode in the midst of a century in which progress was changing the face of Europe. Napoleon III's reign was transitional in many respects, resting a bit uncomfortably between the passions unleashed in 1789 and the appalling chasm that opened up in 1914. The might of a unified Germany was born at the expense of Napoleon III, and while this was happening, within France the emperor was trying to evolve a system of power rooted in the nation's past yet flexible enough for its future. Having restored order and respect, he was "crowning the edifice with liberty," as he had promised he would. By authoritarian means, he "saved" France from the socialists and moved society further away from the anarchy and bloody class warfare rampant in 1848. To critics of his methods he could offer the pragmatic needs of the hour. To apprehensions that a Bonapartist empire would bring war, he assured both France and Europe that any empire of his would be an empire of peace. Conquests he had in mind, to be sure, but they were to be in the field of economic and social reform—it was old-fashioned, so he said, for modern states to go to war merely over boundaries or provinces.

Ironically, the empire that was to mean peace was an empire very much involved in war. He did manage, however, to carry through the extensive reforms he had pledged, and the crown he wore merited a particular luster of its own. While modeled after his uncle's, it was nonetheless self-styled and authentic. When autocratic, anti-Napoleonic foreign leaders worried that he wore his imperial dignity because of dynastic succession, his denial left them with an equally discomforting thought: he owed his elevation, not to dynastic inheritance, but to the ballots of a free people. Yet, no amount of rhetoric

1

could divorce his coming to power from the career of Napoleon Bonaparte. He was riveted to men and issues several decades past and nothing could ever change that circumstance. His own work, in turn, was to influence later generations. Europe after his passing was vastly different from Europe before his appearance. It is clear that he was central to much of this transition, but the degree to which he was a causal agent, a catalyst, or simply the victim of forces making for change in his day is a question that has prompted a wide range of historical opinion.

Few prominent figures in modern history are as difficult to categorize or understand as Napoleon III. Many of the problems surrounding the man obtain also to his works, and both have defied objective, adequate assessment. The selections in this booklet represent attempts at such understanding. They approach the following questions: What exactly was Napoleon III's role in the development of French life and institutions? What of his wider impact on European affairs? How does he stand in relation to the First Empire? And what is his importance in the context of twentieth-century developments?

Napoleon III encouraged the study of history largely as a matter of practical politics. The history he regarded as the most meaningful for his time was, of course, the period of the First Empire. In the career of his uncle he found both his example and his program, and in his own historical writing, especially in the two-volume *Life of Julius Caesar,* he tried to demonstrate that these struck a universal chord. Thus when other historians began to evaluate Napoleon III, it was virtually inevitable that he should be measured against the career to which he himself had called so much attention. At the same time, since much of the first Napoleon's fame rested on how he altered and adapted the work of the republican revolutionaries who preceded him, it was only natural to examine how Napoleon III stood in relation to both the First and Second Republics. What kind of steward did Napoleon III prove to be for Liberty, Equality, and Fraternity? After the smoke of Sedan ended his reign and another republic groped its way into existence, the question was particularly relevant—although objectivity regarding the emperor and his work was to be a rare commodity for some time.

As could have been expected, much of the historical writing on Napoleon III has been characterized by a republican bias. Republican historians and friends of constitutional democracy generally have been unable to see much of virtue or integrity in the programs of nineteenth-century conservative and authoritarian leaders. For decades men like Metternich and Nicholas I were presented as merely narrow obstructionists, spokesmen for vested interests, blocking the spread of republican ideals. For these writers "Caesarism" was particularly abhorrent. Taking their cues from Karl Marx, Victor Hugo, or Arthur W. Kinglake, they have portrayed the emperor as essentially a "little" Napoleon, a fumbling enemy and destroyer of republican institutions. Instead of an empire that meant peace, as he had promised, his regime promoted war—the sacred principles of Liberty, Equality, and Fraternity in his hands gave way to Cavalry, Infantry, and Artillery. In our first selection, Albert Guérard provides a first-hand view of the hostile climate of opinion regarding Napoleon III that existed during the early years of the Third Republic. Guérard believed, however, that by the 1940s "practically every critical historian" regarded Napoleon III with "respect and sympathy." How accurate Guérard really was in this regard may be judged from reading L. B. Namier and a number of the selections that follow. To what extent has the hostile orientation survived? Are there any indictments of Napoleon III's "Caesarism" in the other writers? Has the passage of decades changed the republican criticisms in any of its essentials, or have they been merely refined, with vitriolic indictments sobered a bit by measured language but with no real tempering of the basic charges?

Another brand of historical writing appearing during the Third Republic was largely apologetic. Written to counteract the work of republican critics, it followed earlier models and likewise has found later echoes. Here, too, the excesses in language usage were to give way to more objective sounding terminology, but the message remained. Guérard may be thought of as one of these echoes and possibly Theodore Zeldin as well. Do they effectively reply to the republican criticisms? Virtually all of the authors of the following selections have personally passed judgment on Napoleon III, and each has written from a clearly evident orientation. Very few writers on the Second Empire catalogue "the facts" without evaluating them, and failures to judge are rarely covered by façades of objectivity. However, can you find any such façades of objectivity obscuring signs of strong bias?

Perhaps the first truly objective study of Napoleon III was written by F. A. Simpson. After his work, more sympathetic accounts and hostile interpretations continued to appear, but they had now been forced into a more dispassionate mold. As illustrated in the selection by René Arnaud, the emperor finally began to receive a measure of real justice from basically unsympathetic historians. At the same time, the Second Empire continued to have its admirers, such as Robert Sencourt and Albert Guérard, who proved to be much less temperate than Simpson. Our excerpts from Gordon Wright and Octave Aubry appear remarkably restrained considering the positive character of their basic interpretations.

Both the hostile republican critics and the enthusiastic imperial apologists have compared Napoleon III with Napoleon I. Some difference of opinion would be expected, but here almost contradictory conclusions exist. While Frederick B. Artz saw Napoleon III as a counterfeit and fraudulent version of Bonapartist achievement, Simpson maintained that the Second Empire was really more important than the First. Sencourt supplemented the latter view, crediting the emperor with finishing work begun by his uncle. The comparisons of these two Napoleons are interesting, but the procedure tells us little more about either man. Perhaps, despite the obvious temptation, the proper yardstick by which to measure Napoleon III is not the career of Napoleon I.

Yet, new perspectives have appeared, and these in turn have given rise to more historical portraits. The birth of the League of Nations gave new poignancy to the emperor's views on the constructive possibilities of such devices as the international conference and the principle of mediation. Also his ideas on nationalism and on the development of nation states in Europe became more attractive. In this context Sencourt argued that Napoleon III was a truly "modern" ruler, and later critics, such as Arnaud, were much softer in their caricatures of the emperor. The careers of Mussolini and Hitler added another line of reasoning (which republicans could easily accept); thus J. Salwyn Schapiro presents Napoleon III as a proto-Fascist. Mussolini viewed as a spiritual descendant of the Second Empire was an interestingly suggestive idea and one aided by the observation that Hitler's career paralleled the emperor's. Going a step further and using the technique of "comparative biography," L. C. B. Seaman put Napoleon III's life-cycle beside Hitler's to find that the methods of the leader of the Third Reich appeared historically akin to practices during the Second Empire. Such a line of analysis surely prompts questioning on the same ground as the earlier comparisons with Napoleon I, and the selections by Roger Williams and Howard C. Payne partially refute this interpretation. However, to have made the charge is to have planted the idea, and while the indictments may appear overdrawn, the voices in defense of the emperor are not quite convincing. The Fascist label is, at the very least, embarrassing, as may be seen in Guérard's excerpt.

The dramatic economic growth in France during the reign of Napoleon III poses its own special questions, which may be probed in the work by Charles Pouthas. We may ask how this progress was related to imperial policies, whether it flowed from capable and farsighted government activity, or whether Napoleon III was simply fortuitous in leading France at that particular moment. Was his autocracy the prerequisite for prosperity? And how did his wars effect the economic progress of France? Were they, perhaps, rather than peace, the true handmaidens to his prosperity? Further queries arise when Pouthas' presentation is seen in light of the interpretation of Napoleon III written by Philip Guedalla.

In the nineteenth century the concept of "world historical individuals" enjoyed considerable currency. Napoleon I seemed to be of this rare breed, and the writing and speeches of Napoleon III further encouraged the idea. Was Napoleon III himself a "world historical individual"? Was he truly a man of destiny? A number of our selections address themselves to this problem and here, as before, we meet a number of strikingly varied judgments. Guedalla presents us with an essentially tragic figure whose destiny was to follow and use a legend. His destiny was merely to come to power; fate neglected to spell out for him an obvious program to follow—thus his regime became one of drift and indecision. In another tragic view, Williams sees the emperor trying to implement eighteenth-century ideas amid the altered conditions of the nineteenth century. In both of these cases we see a figure evoking sympathy, a man whose best impulses were frustrated by an overwhelming destiny that had cast the dice against him. On the other hand, writers have appeared that have found in his career achievements of lasting merit, and Zeldin reminds us that, indeed, the phrase "man of the century" was applied to Napoleon III. How realistic was this appellation considering especially that the nineteenth was the century of Metternich and Bismarck, Charles Darwin and Karl Marx? How convincing are the various selections that present Napoleon III as merely a player in a part already predetermined? How much of a role did fate play? What was his destiny? Could he not have changed his course? Did he *have* to be the Man of December? Did the Man of December also *have* to be the Man of Sedan, as A. J. P. Taylor suggests?

All of the authors in this booklet formed their conclusions well after the Second Empire had receded into the past and also after the ideal of "scientific" history had been accepted. All are presenting fairly explicit interpretations based on the empire seen at a distance and in the context of twentieth-century trends. Each writer provides another perspective on the man and his regime, and by the end of the booklet the reader will have read quite widely among current perspectives on Napoleon III and his Second Empire. Was the emperor really a proto-Fascist? An enlightened despot? A misguided romantic? Merely an opportunist? A cheap and tarnished ghost of Napoleon I? Or was Napoleon I a simple historic prelude to great and concrete accomplishments by Napoleon III? These questions are alive among scholars today, and go to the heart of understanding the Second Empire. They are part of the legacy left us by Napoleon III and a century of scholarship.

Historical study of Napoleon III has suffered from a lack of materials. Destruction of personal and administrative records during the fall of the Second Empire, combined with the emperor's limited correspondence, leave the historian with a relatively small amount of documents to study. Few figures who were as important historically as Napoleon III are as elusive. Thus it is doubtful whether future research will still forever any of the basic lines of thought presented here. As the twentieth century wears on, however, new interpretations may appear. Although current writers are not as emotionally bound up with the Second Empire as authors in the early Third Republic were, they are immersed in the issues of our own day and do tend to project these into their work. While a number of our selections may be placed in this category, those by Artz, Sencourt, Schapiro, and Pouthas illustrate the problem particularly well. Objectivity is especially difficult for the writer when conditions he is describing are suggestive of those of his own time. Here the dichotomy of republican-imperialist apology gives way to the immediacy of the moment, and the Second Empire may be presented in the vocabulary and practices of a later age. When this occurs, is such writing really history? Does it help us to understand Napoleon III? On the other hand, is it not true that to picture the emperor in terms of our twentieth-century perspective is the only perspective we can have and as close to the truth as it is possible for us to get? We really cannot escape our frame of reference. Once we have met all of the various perspectives on our topic, we cannot help but incorporate each into our own view. We may consider Gordon Wright's selection as of particular interest in this context. We can see that with the passage of time and the need for each generation to rewrite history for its own needs, the portrayal of Napoleon III has changed a great deal; but are any of the refined views really any *truer* than earlier versions? Have we improved at all over "Saint-Simon on horseback"?

ALBERT GUÉRARD (1880–1959) was born and educated in France, but most of his teaching career was spent at various colleges in the United States. A distinguished writer, he worked readily with literary themes as well as more orthodox historical topics and deftly explored areas where the two disciplines overlap. The appearance in 1943 of his *Napoleon III* stimulated a considerable amount of careful rethinking of the emperor's career. Re-evaluation of Napoleon III's reign has been underway since the early 1920s, but few writers have been as sympathetic toward the emperor—"affectionate" is perhaps the more appropriate word. Here he tells us of the currents of French opinion about Napoleon III that flourished during his student days, and then he gives us his own considered judgment of the emperor.*

Napoleon III

No figure in history is more sharply defined than that of Napoleon I. But even in his case, man, career, and legend refuse to coincide. It took the formidable turmoil of the Revolution to turn the young Corsican soldier into a general, a Consul, an Emperor. It took the enormous wave of Romanticism to transmute the military autocrat, after his death, into a democratic myth, the new Prometheus. In the minds of even the most painstaking historians, such as Kircheisen, there is no logical relation between the known facts and the epic glow which surrounds them. To the present day, Napoleon is praised for ideals which he combated, or blamed for policies deter-mined before he attained power; and the great conqueror is most famous for his defeats, Egypt, Russia, Waterloo.

Our confusion deepens immeasurably when we approach the taciturn and shadowy figure of his nephew, Napoleon III. Even less than with the first Emperor is it possible to separate the man from his destiny. It would be idle to wonder what Louis Napoleon Bonaparte might have been had not fate made him a prince, for a prince he was born, and he never forgot the fact for a moment. Nor can we think of him apart from the Second Empire, his creation and his *raison d'être*. Man and regime form a single historical entity; each is incon-

* Reprinted by permission of the publishers from Albert Guérard, *Napoleon III*, Cambridge, Mass.: Harvard University Press, Copyright 1953, by the President and Fellows of Harvard College.

ceivable without the other.

But the Empire is no easier to define than the Emperor. It was an adventure; it was a political system; it was a period. And that period evokes many things in our minds: two harsh glittering decades between the Coup d'État and Sedan, the sudden expansion of industry, the birth and conflict of nationalities, republican ideals struggling against despotism, science at war with religion, Romanticism wounded, Realism triumphant. The scene of history is swept by these contrasting lights; and as they clash or blend they pass over the impassive face of Napoleon III, silent, pathetic, or prophetic, alone for twenty years in the center of the stage.

At the height of his power, they called him the Sphinx of the Tuileries; when he failed, there were many to declare with Bismarck that he was a sphinx without a secret, "a great unfathomed incapacity"; the most indulgent pronounced him a dreamer: three different ways of confessing—or boasting—that one did not understand. With this lazy or supercilious agnosticism we cannot rest satisfied. Yet the sole clue that we have to offer is no whit more scientific: *Chance.* In 1848, the world was out of joint, torn between irreconcilable desires. Louis Napoleon was likewise compounded of all contrasts: epigone and pioneer, tortuous and single-minded, a damaged soul and a humanitarian, a Utopist who kept watch over the money bags. Above all, he was the heir to a legend itself a living chaos. Through one of the great accidents in history, legend, personality, and time met in miraculous accord. Louis Napoleon was, in strict literalness, the man of the hour.

He proved not unworthy of his luck: 1848, 1851, 1856, 1859—after eleven years he was still a mystery and a paradox, the Protean center of a Protean age, with

something in him that peered and strained beyond immediate needs. But the continued miracle demanded continued energy, and the man grew sick. Then everything that his luck, his prestige, his gentle and secret obstinacy had held together began falling apart. For another decade, momentum carried forward the hybrid regime with the ailing man at the helm. Tragically, he was paralyzed, but he was not blind. Then the abrupt end.

We are aware that chance—which Napoleon I called destiny and Napoleon III, more piously, Providence—is no explanation. The only excuse for making it our working hypothesis is that it describes, if it does not explain, the one central fact in Louis Napoleon's career: the spontaneous and quasi-universal acclaim which, in December 1848, turned an obscure pretender into the head of the French state. Although summed up in a single word which is a confession of ignorance, our hypothesis recognizes, and challenges us to examine, the complexity both of the epoch and of the man. It embraces, if it does not reconcile, the three interpretations which are usually offered of the Second Empire and its enigmatic ruler.

The first is the most damaging, and, because of its loose simplicity, the most widely spread and the most ineradicable. It was best expressed, perhaps, by Alexander William Kinglake, the historian of the Crimean War: "It will presently be necessary to contract the field of vision, and going back to the winter of 1851, to glance at the operations of a small knot of middle-aged men who were pushing their fortunes in Paris." A band of adventurers, Persigny, Morny, Maupas, Saint-Arnaud, with the Napoleonic name as their single asset, secured power for their chief through trickery and violence, and maintained themselves for eighteen years through force and fraud. Loot was their sole object; the Empire was not a regime, it was a racket. This version was for many years good Republican orthodoxy in France. Victor Hugo had clothed it with imperishable beauty in his lyric satire *Les Châtiments;* Gambetta repeated it sixteen years later, with the mighty rumble of his southern rhetoric, made more impressive with echoes from Sallust, Cicero, Caesar, and Corneille; decked out with puns and quips, it was Henri Rochefort's only stock-in-trade. It was perfect party propaganda: the imperial villain alone was responsible for Sedan, and the birth of the new Republic was the triumph of virtue....

This conception explains much. What it fails to take into account is the origin of Louis Napoleon's power, the triumphant election of December 1848, before the pretender knew any of the "gang" except Persigny. It chooses to ignore eighteen years of well-planned and solid prosperity, so solid that it stood the test of a disastrous war, and remained a golden memory for two generations. And when Kinglake virtuously avers that "in France, for the most part, the gentlemen of the country resolved to stand aloof from the Government," he does not add that Albert the Good and Victoria became not merely the formal allies but the personal friends of the usurper.

The second interpretation admits that, back of the Coup d'État, there was a principle, and not merely personal greed. That principle may be called *Bonapartism.* Bonapartism is not Napoleonism: the core of it is not martial glory, but material order. Those who hailed the Bonapartist coups d'état of the 18th of Brumaire and the 2nd of December yearned for tranquillity, not for conquest. When anarchy threatens, property demands a strong government and offers the crown to the most efficient police-man; this is called "saving Society." If the policeman, the Man on Horseback, receives the blessing of the Church, his effectiveness will be enhanced. But first of all he must control the regular army, against the army of disorder which naturally congregates in the great industrial centers. The army's avowed purpose, which is to defend the nation's honor and heritage, the soldier's tradition of heroism, the dazzling show of flags, uniforms, decorations, the blare of military bands, barely disguise the essential fact that the troops are a vast police force in reserve. A firm hand, disorder repressed, prosperity restored: a formula which legitimately appeals to the conservative mind. It was for many years that of Porfirio Díaz and his *científicos.* On a loftier plane, it was also the key to the success of Henry IV. For, with his shrewd and kindly smile, the good King would often allude to "the big stick which brings peace." Henry IV, however, was a sovereign by right divine; the ruler who is frankly the head of the police has no such spiritual prestige. So the curse of materialism attaches to Napoleon III and his regime: material order, material prosperity, material pleasures, summed up in the word Bonapartism.

The third interpretation is the one which Louis Napoleon himself offered, in his pamphlets when he was a pretender, in his addresses when he became President and Emperor; we have no right to ignore it. His threefold program was strikingly different from that of the constitutional monarchy and its heir, the Parliamentary Republic. In politics, he stood for Caesarism: democracy incarnated in one man, a national leader above classes and parties, ruling "by the grace of God and the will of the people," pledged to the protection of order, but not of privilege. In the social and economic field, he held that the first duty of the state is not so much to defend vested interests or maintain free competition as to improve the condition of the masses. In international affairs, his aim was friendly coöperation among free nationalities. His purposes were distorted and thwarted in application; and so they are often dismissed as insincere promises, vague Utopias and at best fumbling velleities. This, however, is sheer partisanship. A direct study of his record has led many historians to a more favorable conclusion. In eighteen years he achieved much. It was his hope that humanitarian Caesarism would grow under the protection of Bonapartism, and ultimately supplant it. Material order, for him, was not an all-sufficient end, but only a condition of progress.

Racketeer, policeman, reformer: no student of the period will deny that all three elements were mingled in that equivocal figure. As to their relative importance, no consensus prevails. It must be noted as a fact, however, that the hostile legend, the Kinglake–Hugo–Gambetta–Rochefort tradition, survives only in the shallower books. The character and work of Napoleon III still offer baffling problems; but invariably the result of intimate study is to increase our sympathy and our respect.

This was my own experience. At this point, I am compelled to introduce a personal element. No one believes in the automatic and irreformable "verdict of history." History, even when it is, as Leopold von Ranke would have it, the plain recital of "how it actually happened," is bound to be a selection and an organization of the facts; this implies an interpretation, and the interpretation presupposes an interpreter. Not egotism, but scientific scruple, should prompt the writer to measure his own personal equation, the inevitable

aberration of his mental instrument.

I was brought up in the purest Republican faith. I learned my letters in the books of Victor Hugo, and my father always referred to the Emperor by the old contemptuous nickname "Badinguet." In that faith I lived undisturbed until I reached manhood. The first scholarly histories of Napoleon III had already appeared—Pierre de la Gorce's, Thirria's—but I was not aware of their existence. When Dechartre, in Le Lys Rouge, referred to the Emperor as "an affectionate soul," and praised "his simple courage, his gentle fatalism," I smiled understandingly, for I knew that Anatole France reveled in outrageous paradoxes.

The change came slowly. Its instruments were not books or men, but the streets of my native Paris. I came to realize that the Paris we know best, and which hundreds of cities have sought to emulate, is the work of Baron Haussmann; and I discovered the plain truth that Haussmann was but the agent of Napoleon III himself. The faults of Haussmann's work are obvious. It suffers from excessive symmetry and monotony, emphasized rather than relieved by the questionable taste of a few public buildings. Even in my childhood, my favorite nooks were those which had escaped the pickaxe of the formidable Prefect. Yet I did feel then, as I do now, that the transformation of Paris under the Second Empire was nobly planned. The mind that conceived it must have been far-sighted, generous, and bold.

From 1908 to 1912, I was engaged in a study of religious thought in French literature under the Second Empire. I could not escape the conclusion that the whole period had been maligned. We had chosen to remember only its frivolousness, as though Offenbach and Princess Pauline Metternich were the typical

French people of the age. We had forgotten that solid works of religious philosophy were not merely written in those days, but discussed with passionate earnestness. I had vaguely believed that all serious literature was in opposition or in exile; I came to realize that, with the exception of Hugo and Quinet, the best writers under the "Tyranny" lived and labored at home in perfect freedom.

My purpose had not been to study political conditions and least of all the person of the sovereign. But through the rich memoirs and letters of the time I found that Napoleon III could not be ignored. Many of the leaders in literature—Mérimée, Gautier, Augier, Flaubert, Sainte-Beuve, George Sand, Taine, Renan—had friends among the members of the imperial family. The poet whose art and thought I respected most, Alfred de Vigny, admired the Emperor. The simple and courageous testimony of Louis Pasteur, on the morrow of Sedan, impressed me deeply. Not from a single source, but from innumerable allusions and chance remarks, a new figure of Napoleon III was formed in my mind. The elderly rake in the uniform of a policeman, heavy-lidded, with dyed hair, goatee, and long waxed moustaches, melted into the gentle character described by Dechartre in *Le Lys Rouge,* and painted by Hippolyte Flandrin. In reading those innumerable volumes, I found that no one had ever approached him—whatever his prejudices might be, foreign ruler, diplomat or soldier, Republican, scholar, man of the people, Queen Victoria, Francis Joseph, Victor Duruy, Émile Ollivier, Louis Pasteur—without being won over by his profound and unaffected kindliness.

This personal appreciation did not in the least affect my political ideas. I never was tempted for a moment to turn Bonapartist, even in retrospect. I have retained to this day my admiration for Victor Hugo, not only as a poet, but as a man. In Hugo's mind and character there were elements which, if not base, were at any rate common; but he had also the fierce righteous anger, the magnificent and somber imagination of a Hebrew prophet. In his resistance to the Coup d'État he may have been pragmatically mistaken, but he was morally right. He struck superb attitudes of defiance; but, however theatrical, they were none the less inspired by his conscience. Of the two, the Emperor was by far the more civilized. He had a gentler soul, a more practical sensitiveness to human suffering, a more intelligent interest in modern technique as an instrument of human welfare. But Hugo, in the garb of a shrewd French bourgeois, was a weird primitive seer, and transcends the ages.

Three quarters of a century have elapsed since Napoleon III disappeared from the European scene. Yet the Second Empire, so remote in some of its aspects, is in its essence strangely modern and indeed contemporary. Our world begins in 1848. There were many men under Louis Philippe who had never taken a railroad journey, and many for whom manhood suffrage or socialism were ludicrous Utopian dreams. But the problems of eighty and ninety years ago are with us still. Marx, Darwin, Wagner, are living forces, and their doctrines are living issues. The books, pamphlets, speeches of that time could be given out today. The wave of the future, whatever it may mean, was battling against the shores of Europe nearly a century ago; and we are not certain that it has gained even one painful inch.

To this, not to its tarnished tawdriness, gay uniforms, and crinolines, does the Second Empire owe its fascination. It is the present, but the present with a perspective. It makes us aware of dangers, but also of opportunities, which we might overlook in the weariness of our daily toil. History is experience; it broadens the field of contemporary politics; and, like all experience, it does not preclude experiment.

The reverse process is no less legitimate and no less inevitable; the present throws a light upon the past. This does not mean that we should inject the quarrels of one age into the problems of another. Partisanship is never justified, and in this case, we need particularly to be on our guard. We are living in an age of conflict, and many believe that one-sidedness, which they mistake for wholeheartedness, is the essential condition of victory. This delusion might lead us to condemn in the past anything which resembles what we hate in the present. Between the origins and principles of the Second Empire and those of the Nazi regime there are striking similarities. In both cases, a great nation was chafing under a *Diktat*.... In both cases, there was a desire to avenge a defeat and to reconquer historical frontiers. In both, there was utter disgust with the bewilderment and impotence of Parliamentary rule. In both, there was an appeal to the vast conservative lower middle class against the "Red Specter," Communism. In both, there was a bid for the support of the masses, by offering them a bolder social program than the Parliamentarians had dared to envisage. In both, the political formula was Caesarian Democracy; a single leader endorsed by a plebiscite.

These resemblances cannot fail to be present in the reader's mind, as they are in my own. History is not mere chronology: it records the conflict of principles, the clash of sentiments, the competition of interests. If we were to ignore such factors, history would be a dead

mass of meaningless documents; but as soon as we strive to understand them, we seem to be making a case for them, and our impartiality is impugned. I can affirm that my purpose is strictly nonpartisan; but I know that such a claim is the commonest among students of history, and the hardest to sustain. I am seeking to present Napoleon III as I understand him. I have no desire to use him as a whipping boy to chastise Hitler, as, under the Second Empire, the opposition used Tiberius of Rome and Soulouque of Haiti. Still less is it my intention to offer an indirect apology for the ruthless German dictatorship, or for the pathetic Vichy regime....

"The Emperor may await with confidence the judgment of posterity. His reign will remain among the most glorious in our history." These words written by Louis Pasteur in a glow of indignation and despair will be read by most with a pitying, melancholy smile. At the close of this study, upon which I have been engaged for thirty years, I have no hope of altering the verdict of the unthinking. Legends, it seems, are indestructible. To the end of time, people will believe that William Tell did shoot the apple; that Frederick the Great was the incarnation of the German national spirit and the hero of the Protestant faith; that Napoleon I was the crowned soldier of the Revolution, a good European, and invincible on the battlefield; that Bismarck was a flawless realist; and that Karl Marx, single-handed, transformed Socialism from vague Utopia into rigorous science. In this world of unchallenged convention, Napoleon III stands irremediably condemned.

If we pass from loose tradition to careful research, the scene changes altogether. Within the last fifty years, Napoleon III has won the respect and sympathy of practically every critical historian. The old Carlylean tone of contempt is found only in popular works or textbooks at third or fourth hand. Even the frankly biased account by the *petit bourgeois* Radical Charles Seignobos, a period piece of the Gambetta age, and that by Albert Thomas in an orthodox "Socialist" series are completely different in tone from the apocalyptic vituperations of Victor Hugo.

On the other hand, I hate the word *glorious* which Pasteur applied to the reign of Napoleon III.... In the Napoleonic sense of martial fame, we had better forget *glory* altogether. The Crimean War was a costly blunder; Napoleon III himself was horror-stricken on the battlefields of Italy, and whatever sickly laurels he may have won fell to dust at Sedan. If *glory* evokes gorgeous display, the glittering Court, the gay uniforms, the gilded Grand Opera, behold, this also is vanity. All this tarnished splendor has acquired with the years a kind of baroque charm, futile and pathetic; but it is appealing only because it is dead.

What Pasteur had in mind, the true *glory* of Napoleon III, is that he was profoundly devoted to the cause of the masses, the inarticulate, the humble, the forgotten. This was his "democracy," his "socialism," a deeper reality than any constitutional form or any pseudo-scientific doctrine. In this he stands almost unique in the long line of French sovereigns. In comparison, the truly *glorious* rulers, Francis I, Richelieu, Louis XIV, Napoleon I, are cold and harsh; they prized France merely as their pedestal. Only three kings are remembered because there was in them a touch of tenderness for the common folk: Louis XII was called "the Father of the People," but he has become very shadowy; Louis XVI said to Turgot, "You and I alone love

the people"—but his good will was a feeble reed; Henry IV is still a cherished memory, and most of all perhaps for his homely slogan, "A chicken in the pot every Sunday." In his early career, Henry of Navarre was even more of an adventurer than Louis Napoleon; when he came to power, he did not grant France any "liberties" of the Parliamentary kind; and he was no paragon of puritanical virtue. Yet to many readers, the comparison will seem absurd: Henry remains a universal favorite, the frank admirers of Napoleon III are few and apologetic. Why this difference? First of all, Henry was murdered—a great boon. Then, in those days, there were bitter factions but no organized parties; so his successors, while reversing his policies, did not find it essential to blacken his memory. And, above all, Henry had the advantage of *style*. He might be frivolous, but he was bluff and hearty. He was, in the words of the old song, "the triple-threat man, who could drink, fight, and make love," all with a delightful touch of bravado. He was "French of the French," if your ideal of France is to be found in Alexandre Dumas rather than in Alfred de Vigny. Napoleon III had no dash and very little humor; he was gentleness and silence. Yet he too was recognized by the people as their friend and their leader.

His faith in the people, his desire to serve the people, assumed a threefold form. In European affairs, it became *the principle of nationalities,* the right of self-determination ascertained by plebiscites. In the economic and social field, it manifested itself as *Saint-Simonian socialism:* order and prosperity, for the purpose of improving the welfare of the most numerous and poorest class. In politics, it sought realization as *direct democracy,* brushing aside those intermediate powers which invariably bolster privilege.

Upon the first two articles of his faith, we shall insist no more. He was a better European than Bismarck or Gambetta, and a better socialist than Karl Marx, because he was less narrow than they, and not poisoned with hatred and pride. The things he labored for, confusedly, haltingly, shall come to pass if this war is not to be eternal: all nationalities free and equal within a United Europe, industrial wealth for the service of the many, not for the profit of the few. These were Utopias yesterday; they are at this hour the only alternative to strife and chaos. The third part of his creed, direct democracy, is more controversial. Rightly understood, it might be his most substantial contribution to the making of modern Europe.

The ideal of Napoleon III was a national, non-partisan government. This conception is sharply opposed to the multi-party system, which is the foundation of all Parliamentary regimes; and it is even more directly antagonistic to the single-party system, which is Totalitarianism. Strictly speaking, until the fall of the Empire, Bonapartism was not a party.

The State, according to this view, represents only those interests which cannot be divided without destruction, and in which every one, whatever his private opinions may be, necessarily has a share. These can be summed up in one word, *security:* international security, which, ideally, means a just and durable peace, and, immediately, national defense; security at home, that is to say law and order. Its necessary instrument is a disciplined force, the army and the police. The head of the State, not for glory, but for service, is a man in uniform. This collective security should be above controversy: *Salus populi suprema lex*

esto. The secondary task of the government is to promote *general* prosperity, through those improvements which do not exclusively serve private interests—public works, the development of natural resources. Whatever is factional or sectional is not the proper domain of the State; the government should be, not the agent of a victorious party, but the *greatest common denominator* of all private interests.

Security, order, prosperity, are strictly material ends. The government which limits itself to their service is frankly a materialistic government. These things, by definition, are Caesar's. All that we can reasonably demand of Caesar is that he should perform his restricted task honestly and well. We should not expect the police or the postal authorities to be idealistic; their sole duty is to be non-partisan and to be efficient.

Saint-Simonian socialism, generously Utopian as it appears, is yet in perfect harmony with this materialistic conception of the State. If the aim of the State is the *common* good, if the State be indeed a *commonwealth,* leaving private interests to private initiative, then automatically it will be devoted to "the welfare of the most numerous class," which is also the poorest. Those who are above that common level do not need the State; they can take care of themselves. In concrete terms, it is the business of the State to prevent famine, but not to provide luxuries. It should "extinguish pauperism": it should not seek to create millionaires. So long as millionaires can grow richer without causing destitution, the State does not interfere with them. But if there be a connection between luxury at one end and famine at the other, then the State has the right and the duty to move. The common good, the good of the common man, must first be served.

This conception of the State as above parties is recognized to a large extent in the most orthodox of Parliamentary regimes. We deprecate partisanship even in elected office holders: a Mayor should be the Mayor of the city, not of the victorious faction. The spoils system is the natural consequence of the party spirit, for if all men must take sides, solidly, for the Blacks or the Greens, and if the other side is necessarily wrong in all things, then it is our duty to "turn the rascals out"—generals, engineers, and judges as well as governors, sheriffs, and dog-catchers. Yet we are now ashamed of the spoils system, and we are striving to eliminate it from public administration. In a crisis such as war, we have no doubt that common interests must take unquestioned precedence. Now the State should consider itself as constantly at war; not against other States—such a criminal thought never guided Napoleon III—but against disorder, disease, and want. Within that sphere, and for the duration of that eternal fight, there should be no parties.

Napoleon III was not averse to parties because he had an autocratic temperament: on the contrary, no one could be more considerate in his relations with other men, and even with dogs. He condemned parties because, in his opinion, they had irremediable faults. Even when they were perfectly honest, their squabbles paralyzed necessary action; this had been evident under Louis Philippe and the Second Republic. But could they ever be perfectly honest? Parties are inconceivable without partisanship, which is the deliberate warping of one's thought. If a man seeks to remain impartial and free, he cannot commit himself to any party organization. Worst of all, party rule, if logically carried out, is of necessity tyrannical. The party in power attempts to impose its full program upon the defeated. To be sure, the minority hopes to conquer power in its turn; party government is thus a series of wrongs offset by other wrongs, which is an extremely wasteful method of never attaining the right. These are not the excesses of the party spirit, but its very essence. The only legitimate field of government action should be the nonpartisan.

If we could afford to be as paradoxical as Einstein, we should say that this field is restricted, yet indefinitely extensible. The *greatest common denominator* may grow. We have attempted to show that Napoleon III did not believe in the "minimal State" of the philosophical anarchists. It was with him an article of faith that the government should not be defensive merely, but positive, dynamic, an instrument for the common good. In him, the policeman and the humanitarian were not at odds. The "guardian of the peace" was also an agent of progress.

But, if the sphere of the government is constantly expanding, there ever remains a domain beyond: the free, boundless, teeming domain of opinions—religious, social, political, artistic. So long as a thought is merely an *opinion,* even if it be passionately held by a majority, it has no right to turn itself into a *law,* binding upon the minority. Most Americans are Christians; a majority of them are Protestants. They have steadily refused to establish a State religion, or to make their creed part of the Constitution, for, by so doing, they would be outlawing dissenters, depriving Jews, Buddhists, or agnostics of their full citizenship. *There are things that are not Caesar's.* This Napoleon III fully understood, and therein lies the radical difference between his democracy and modern dictatorships. For *they* believe in the single-party system, imposing its will upon all dwellers in the land and in every domain, the ideal as well as the material. Not only must men, under their rule, obey the same traffic regulations, but they must think and feel alike, or else they are crushed into silence.

Beyond the expanding *greatest common denominator* of security, order, prosperity, the regime of Napoleon III was definitely pluralistic. It did not matter that the Empress should be at heart a Legitimist, Morny an Orleanist, Prince Napoleon a Republican, and the Emperor himself a Socialist: if they obeyed the law and sought to promote the general welfare, they could be faithful servants of the community. Persigny, because he was a *mere* Bonapartist, was properly voted crazy. Pluralism is not identical with liberty—one might conceive of pluralistic tyrannies existing side by side—but it is the indispensable condition of liberty. The country which seeks to impose spiritual unity, by forcible or insidious means, is not free. Authority, on the other hand, is not antagonistic to liberty. The police is the protector of our innermost freedom; it makes it possible for us to differ in peace.

The Empire prohibited political meetings almost up to the end, because it was frankly committed to the suppression of factional strife. It did not abolish the liberty of the press; the blunders of a few policemen and censors should not blind us to that essential fact. Journalists were made responsible for misstatements and personal insults, but throughout the Empire there were papers which were openly Legitimist, Orleanist, Republican, anticlerical, or Ultramontane in their sympathies. Prévost-Paradol, who opposed the Empire until 1870, recognized as early as 1853 that the result of "the Tyranny" was actually to raise the intellectual and literary level of discussion. Vociferations were discouraged; in-

controvertible facts stated with moderation had a chance to be heard; criticism could be sharp and even bitter, if it remained courteous. Those keen-edged weapons, allusion and irony, recovered a favor and an effectiveness they had lost since the days of Voltaire. The fearless expression of delicate thought has two enemies: the dead silence imposed by a despot, the universal tumult of full license; the second is the worse. Not merely expression, but thought itself is drowned by competitive bellowing; in the stillness of a jail, a man can at least hear himself think. The Second Empire was neither a jail nor a pandemonium; men could reflect, and talk.

More deadly to liberty than any censor are respectable conventions, unchallenged conformities. In Victorian England, wrote Hilaire Belloc, "a sort of cohesive public spirit glued and immobilized all individual expression. One could float imprisoned as in a stream of thick substance, one could not swim against it." The public spirit of the Second Empire was not cohesive, and that is why its activity was so intense and so many-sided. Never, not even in the great moments of the Renaissance and the Enlightenment, were *all* schools of thought so vigorously represented. Within the solid framework of the materialistic state, the richest spiritual anarchy prevailed; and in that domain, anarchy should be the only law. Many years ago, in *French Prophets of Yesterday,* I attempted to catalogue that unexampled surge of intellectual energy. But no critical guide can do full justice to a period in which Catholics and Protestants of all shades, Humanitarians, Free-thinkers, Voltairian Rationalists, Saint-Simonians, Positivists, mystics, devil-worshippers, scientists, anarchists, socialists, believers in Art for Art's Sake, went fearlessly to the end of their thought.

"Frivolous" France under the Second Empire could be amused by fancy-dress balls, by grand reviews in dashing uniforms, by Offenbach operettas, by the sauciness of Theresa or the antics of Princess Metternich, by the light wit of Alphonse Karr, Aurélien Scholl, Albert Wolff, Arsène Houssaye, Paul de Kock, Henri Rochefort, Meilhac and Halévy. But, with the hubbub of politics almost completely hushed, she could also be stirred, as we are not, by philosophical and religious controversy. A lecture by Renan at the Collège de France was an event of national importance. His *Life of Jesus,* quiet and scholarly, gave rise at once to hundreds of passionate attacks and defenses. There were police regulations, but no taboos. No cranny of human experience was left unexplored. And under that apparent chaos, there ruled a deep and definite hierarchy of values.

Napoleon III was, to borrow Gamaliel Bradford's phrase, a "damaged soul"; and, after 1860, a damaged soul imprisoned in a damaged body. Grave, thoughtful, kind, devoted to noble causes, determined withal, fearless, and surprisingly practical, he had in him also the tortuousness of the eternal plotter, the vagueness of the Utopian, the weakened fiber of the sensualist, the fatalism of the gambler. Some characters in history are obvious in their greatness, mediocrity, or turpitude: even though our sympathies may widely differ, we feel that we can focus Washington, Victoria, Gladstone, and even Napoleon I. Napoleon III is not one of these. His elusive physiognomy changes altogether with the light that is turned upon it. At one moment, he appears impressive; the only political leader in the nineteenth century whose thought could still be a guide for us today. At other times, the carica-

ture drawn by Kinglake and Victor Hugo seems almost convincing: the middle-aged rake in imperial trappings, sinister even in his futility. The most searching, the most persistent light of all, the one in which he was seen by every one who approached him, reveals him as gentle, not merely in speech and smile, but to the very depths of his being.

And the unique regime he fashioned was no less enigmatic: strangely attractive, not in its glitter, not even in its daring, but in its "humanity," yet damaged also, and from the very first. The Roman Expedition in 1849, the fusillade on the fourth of December 1851, were causes of confusion not wholly dispelled to this day. They inflicted upon Caesarian Democracy as Louis Napoleon conceived it wounds which at the end of twenty years still refused to heal. In addition to these tragic accidents, there were antinomies in the very structure of the Empire which made its survival precarious. The most obvious, however, was only apparent: the conflict between authority and liberty. Neither of these principles can cover the whole of life, and the Empire, more clearly than other regimes, defined their respective spheres. More dangerous was the Napoleonic heritage; a government which was modern, peace-minded, democratic, industrial, socialistic, grew out of the "Legend," which was the crude exaltation of military adventure. Napoleon III was entirely different from Napoleon I, whom he had used purely as a Promethean myth; but so long as the Bonapartes ruled, it would have been hopeless to eliminate the Napoleonic virus—as hopeless at it was for Prussia to cast off the ruthless cynicism of Frederick the Great. There are forms of ingratitude that history will not tolerate: you cannot build upon the glory of the Founder and then denounce that glory as a thing of evil.

This leads us to the fatal flaw in the Empire, the restoration of heredity. Louis Napoleon was not fully conscious of the contradiction it implied. His thought was a unique historical complex, and he sincerely believed that his blood, his tradition, his doctrine, and the will of the people were in miraculous harmony: *vox populi* and *vox Dei,* in unison, would inevitably utter the same word, *Napoleon*. This mystic delusion was at one time shared by many; but a delusion it was, and could not endure. Yet for the first twenty years of his political career, Louis Napoleon resisted the temptation. His first "Dream of a Constitution" (*Rêveries politiques*) in 1832, and the definite project he submitted to the people in 1851, provided for an elected Chief of State.

Had he gave up power at the end of ten years, according to his own proposal, his term of office, although far from flawless, would have justified the highest praise. Heredity is a harmless fiction if the sovereign is but a figurehead; it becomes an absurdity if he attempts to be the active and responsible leader of the nation. Because the dynastic Empire had been restored, France had to submit, after 1861, to the rule of a man intelligent no doubt, well-meaning, experienced, but ailing, and unable to exercise for good the power he still claimed to wield. She might have been autocratically governed, in the name of a child, by a high-spirited but narrow-minded woman. She might have been exposed to the uncongenial and capricious dictatorship of Prince Napoleon. If, on the other hand, Napoleon III had yielded in time, if he had accepted in 1863–64 the offer of Adolphe Thiers and restored a Parliamentary monarchy, he would have become a mere Louis Philippe in gaudier trappings; he would

have sacrificed the principle which was his *raison d'être,* Caesarian democracy.

History is not chemistry; there is no method that will enable us to analyze with irrefutable definiteness the elements of a complex situation. We have tried honestly to do so, and we are aware that the result cannot be called scientific knowledge. There entered into the making of Louis Napoleon's career accidents, a personality, and a principle; heterogeneous as they were, they remain indissolubly fused.

It is with the principle that we are chiefly concerned. That principle is *direct democracy*. The experiment failed, not because the principle could be proved wrong, but because it was not applied in its full and honest simplicity. Caesarism reverted to heredity; the opposition, of the Right and of the Left, was bent on restoring factional strife, as if that alone deserved the name of Liberty. Three forces united in raising Louis Napoleon to supreme power: the Imperial Legend, the dread of disorder, and humanitarian democracy. All three were very real, but the third was the deepest in French opinion, and in Louis Napoleon's own soul. The regime which he conceived resembles the American far more than it does British Parliamentarism on the one hand, Totalitarian Dictatorship on the other. It might be well for France, when she resumes the normal course of her destiny, to borrow her inspiration from the United States rather than from England. If she did so, the Constitution of 1852 would be for her a better starting point than the Constitution of 1875. And she would be fortunate indeed if she found again, under such a regime, a leader with the unfailing gentleness, the quiet intellectual courage, the profound generosity, of Napoleon III.

One of Great Britain's most distinguished and perceptive historians, SIR LEWIS B. NAMIER (1888–1960) taught and carried on his research first at Balliol College, Oxford, and then at the University of Manchester. A specialist in diplomatic and political history, his contributions to scholarship on George III and also on the revolutions of 1848 have had a dramatic impact. In the article below, Namier addresses himself directly to the portrait of Napoleon III which Guérard had drawn. His incisive analysis is particularly effective because it provides a challenging antidote to such writing as that of Guérard. Namier's view of Napoleon III is especially unflattering and an example of a line of thought still current regarding the emperor.*

The First Mountebank Dictator

With Napoleon I things were serious and real ... he raised no bogies and whipped up no passions; he aimed at restoring sanity and at consolidating the positive results of the Revolution; and if, in superposing the Empire on the Republic and in recreating a Realm of the West, he evoked the memories of Caesar and Charlemagne, the appeal was decorative rather than imitative. There would have been no occasion for his dictatorship had not the living heritage of French history been obliterated by revolution; but his system has left its own unhealthy legend, a jackal-ghost which prowls in the wake of the "Red spectre." Napoleon III and Boulanger were to be the plagiarists, shadowy and counterfeit, of Napoleon I; and Mus-

solini and Hitler were to be unconscious reproducers of the methods of Napoleon III. For these are inherent in plebiscitarian Caesarism, or so-called "Caesarian democracy," with its direct appeal to the masses: demagogical slogans; disregard of legality in spite of a professed guardianship of law and order; contempt of political parties and the parliamentary system, of the educated classes and their values; blandishments and vague, contradictory promises for all and sundry; militarism; gigantic, blatant displays and shady corruption. . . .

The first coups of Louis-Napoleon, at Strasbourg in 1836 and at Boulogne in 1840, were miserable failures, like Hitler's Munich *Putsch* of 1923. Both men were treated with humane and neglect-

* Reprinted from Sir Lewis Namier, *Vanished Supremacies* (London, 1958), by permission of Hamish Hamilton, Inc.

ful forbearance, and in the enforced leisure of their comfortable prisons they composed their programmatic works— *Des Idées Napoléoniennes* and *Mein Kampf*. Not even at a later stage did the political leaders realize the full gravity of the situation—thinking in terms of their own and not in those of the masses, they could not descry either in Louis-Napoleon or in Hitler a possible ruler or dictator. Louis-Napoleon escaped from his prison at Ham in 1846, and settled in London. On the outbreak of the February Revolution he hastened to Paris, a professed supporter of the Republic; but when requested by the Provisional Government to leave the country, he complied. . . . "When one is weak, one has to submit and await better days," he wrote to his cousin Napoleon ("Plonplon") in 1844; and on 5th June 1848: "In these moments of exaltation, I prefer to remain in the background." Re-elected in September by five constituencies, he took his seat, and read out a brief address affirming his devotion "to the defence of order and the strengthening of the Republic." "These correct words, spoken in a toneless voice, were received with perfunctory applause," writes his latest biographer, Mr. Albert Guérard. He looked

disarmingly unobtrusive. His torso was long and his legs short; he moved awkwardly, with a shuffling gait; his head sat heavily on his broad and round shoulders; his countenance was pale and immobile; his eyes were small, heavy-lidded, of an undefinable grey. . . . He was not downright ludicrous; he was not exactly commonplace; he certainly was not impressive.

When the Assembly, enmeshed in constitutional doctrine and democratic dogma, decided to have the President of the Republic elected by popular vote, and not by the Legislature, the door was opened for a Bonapartist restoration. To preclude it, an amendment was moved debarring members of former ruling families.

Every eye turned towards Louis-Napoleon, for the amendment was aimed at him alone. He went up to the tribune and, in a few halting sentences, uttered with a strangely un-French accent, he protested against "the calumnies constantly hurled at his head," stammered, ended abruptly and shuffled back to his seat.

The amendment was withdrawn, its mover himself describing it, "after what we have just seen and heard," as superfluous. On 10th December 1848, in the Presidential election, Louis-Napoleon received 5,400,000 votes against 1,800,000 of his four opponents; Lamartine—poet, orator, and leader in the Provisional Government—found himself at the bottom of the poll, with a mere 17,000. . . . "The remote lack-lustre gaze of his grey eyes, now that it was fraught with destiny, could be declared sphinx-like or prophetic," writes Mr. Guérard. And Pierre de La Gorce, historian of the Second Empire, says that the change which success produced in the public estimate of the same traits of Louis-Napoleon's character was like a picture advertising a hair-restorative: "before" and "after." Between these two appraisements, the taciturn, shadowy, impassive figure of Napoleon III has puzzled the century which has gone by, as the shrieking, convulsed, hysterical figure of Hitler will puzzle the one to come. "A sphinx without a riddle," was Bismarck's summing up of Napoleon III; "from afar something, near at hand nothing"; "a great unfathomed incapacity." And N. W. Senior reports Tocqueville having said to him in January 1852:

Louis-Napoleon is essentially a copyist. He can originate nothing; his opinions, his theories, his maxims, even his plots, all are borrowed, and from the most dangerous of models—from a man who, though he possessed genius and industry such as are not seen ... once in a thousand years, yet ruined himself by the extravagance of his attempts.

But Napoleon III, said Grimblot to Senior in 1855, "lacked industry and capacity"—and on this point most contemporaries are agreed.

When we were together in England [continued Grimblot] I saw much of him. We have walked for hours in the Green Park. His range of ideas is narrow, and there is always one which preoccupies him ... and shuts out the others. ... He learns little from his own meditations, for he does not balance opposite arguments; he learns nothing from conversation, for he never listens. ...

And an unnamed friend of Senior's, in 1858: "... as he is ignorant, uninventive, and idle, you will see him flounder from one failure to another." Guizot, Thiers, Montalembert, Falloux, Duvergier de Hauranne, Victor Hugo, Ampère, Beaumont, they all despised *celui-ci;* but the opposition of the intellectuals was tolerated because, as Tocqueville put it, their writings were not read "by the soldier or by the *prolétaire.*" ...

"Within the last fifty years," writes Mr. Guérard, "Napoleon III has won the respect and sympathy of practically every critical historian." Sympathy, perhaps; but respect is based on a man's actions, and not on his dreams and intentions. La Gorce, summing up a life's work, wrote about Napoleon III in 1933: "Baleful *(funeste)* he was: still, hardly have I written the word than I would like to soften it, for he was good and even enlightened; but no sooner did the light break through than it was clouded." Nor does Mr. Guérard's book, the product of years of study, yield a very different result, though the story is often lyricized, especially in an attempt to

represent Napoleon III as a far-sighted reformer, a "Saint-Simon on horseback" whose régime is of the most "vital importance." Moreover praise is offered of his plebiscitarian dictatorship, of "direct democracy" as contrasted with "parliamentary practices." None the less, the picture which emerges of Napoleon III is hardly fit to inspire respect in the reader.

Mr. Guérard seeks "to understand Napoleon III," but finds no solution to the "enigma." "His elusive physiognomy changes altogether with the light that is turned upon it." His mind was "complex, perhaps tortuous"; "perhaps unfathomable, perhaps simply nebulous"; there was "no flash of intuition, no capacity for sudden decision." Princess Mathilde, Louis-Napoleon's cousin and at one time his betrothed, exasperated by his taciturnity, wished she could "break his head, to find out what there is in it"; and both she and her brother, Prince Napoleon, "ascribed his caution to mental hesitancy or flabbiness of will." He had grown up "in an atmosphere of elegiac resignation," writes Mr. Guérard; and in his youth he was "retarded in development, 'gently stubborn,' as his mother called him." He was a "damaged soul." But, like La Gorce, Mr. Guérard stresses Napoleon III's "profound and unaffected kindliness," his gravity, courtesy, and gentleness—"a man of '48," "a democratic humanitarian." In his own eyes Napoleon III was "a providential man," "an instrument of the Divine Purpose"; but even that faith "was 'gently obstinate,' not blatant." "I am sure that the shade of the Emperor protects and blesses me," he wrote from Ham in 1842. Even in his obsessionist ideas he lacked energy and ruthlessness. How then did such a man succeed?

By the time the Napoleonic disaster had assumed "dramatic value and epic grandeur," in the late 'twenties, Roman-

ticism adopted "the Napoleonic theme,"
writes Mr. Guérard; and in the 'thirties
the Emperor turned "into a hero of
folk-lore." The July Monarchy, prosaic
and dull, could not afford to dramatize
conservatism without playing into the
hands of the Legitimists, nor move to
the Left, for fear of the Republicans; but
they tried to surfeit France with Napoleon's glory, "retrospective, and therefore safe." As was proved by Louis-
Napoleon's failure at Boulogne, this was
then "but a legend . . . something to be
enjoyed rather than to be believed in or
acted upon . . . a sufficient motive for a
pageant, but not for a revolution." How
did it ever come to life? Even in the
early months of the Revolution "Bonapartism was advancing . . . with a strict
minimum of ideology, organization, and
expenditure"—"it held itself in reserve."
But had it ever more than a minimum
of ideas and resources? To Mr. Guérard,
Louis-Napoleon is not "merely the pas-
sive heir of the Legend"—he reshaped
it "in his own image" and by his pamphlets
created in the public mind that paradoxical
association between Bonapartism and humanitarian democracy which was Louis-Napoleon's special contribution to politics. It
was not exclusively the Emperor's nephew,
it was also the man who had written *On the
Extinction of Pauperism,* who was chosen
by the people in December 1848.

"The chief quality in Louis-Napo-
leon's style is its directness. . . . His words
are historical documents." Not many
who have read those pamphlets are likely
to endorse such praise. La Gorce says
that they are neither good nor bad, but
significant; turgid, contradictory, and
baffling, both naïve and cunning; they
develop common-places "with a sustained
solemnity"; but occasionally, he claims,
there occurs an original idea. Some of
us have failed to discover any. In fact,

had the electorate been sufficiently advanced to read Louis-Napoleon's writings
fewer might have voted for him—but
what percentage is likely even to have
heard of them?

According to Mr. Guérard, Louis-Napoleon was elected on his own programme of "authoritarian democracy,"
known, understood, and "freely endorsed
by 5,400,000 votes." All political parties
stood for "the privileges of some élite":
with the Legitimists the criterion was
social superiority, with the Orleanists
property, with the Republicans profes-
sion of their creed. Bonapartism, it is
claimed, brushed aside the "intermediate
powers and special interests"—Parliament and plutocracy—in order to realize
the "unformulated doctrine" of the
people: "direct contact between sovereign and masses." This kind of argument formed indeed the stock-in-trade
of Louis-Napoleon. In his *Idées Napoléoniennes* "the tutelary and democratic
power of the plebeian hero . . . who was
the true representative of our revolution" is contrasted with the aristocratic
or oligarchic character of the British Parliamentary system; "aristocracy requires
no chief, while it is in the nature of
democracy to personify itself in one
man." And the Second Empire in its
depreciation of *les anciens partis,* its
strictures on "sectional interests," and its
bombast about the integration of all
truly national interests and "the organization of modern society," is a forerun-
ner of the single-party totalitarianisms.
. . . Of the five names in the Presidential election "Napoleon" alone had
nation-wide currency; in Parliamentary
elections a similar advantage accrued to
the local notables. Louis-Napoleon's person mattered little, his pamphlets even
less, and of his programme only as
much as could be read into his name, a
greater engine of propaganda than even

the modern Press and the wireless. Through the freak of a plebiscite the ghost of Napoleon entered the body politic of a sick, deeply divided community . . . everybody abhorred and feared the "Reds," so much so that even of those who knew Louis-Napoleon in the flesh and despised him—the politicans—many supported him. They thought that because he was intellectually their inferior, they would be able to run him or get rid of him; the German Conservatives—Junkers, industrialists, generals, Nationalists—thought the same about Hitler. "The elect of six millions executes, and does not betray, the will of the people," declared Louis-Napoleon, nicely rounding off the figure. But too much should not be read into that verdict by historians.

"The workmen of the great cities," writes Mr. Guérard, ". . . refused to recognize the Empire as a genuine form of democracy." Their strength and spirit were broken in the June Days of 1848 long before Louis-Napoleon appeared as the "saviour of society" (Cavaignac was his Noske). But exploiting the feeble riots of June 1849, engaged in *par acquit de conscience,* Louis-Napoleon proclaimed: "It is time that the good be reassured, and that the wicked should tremble." And after the *coup d'État* his shady associates staged their own "Reichstag Fire." There had been hardly any opposition, the workers refusing to fight; but as some kind of insurrection was required to justify the coup and extensive repressions, resistance was encouraged and beaten down. Next, an accidental shot on the boulevards provoked a fusillade; the ground was strewn with dead. "These were not insurgents," writes Mr. Guérard; "it was a quiet, well-dressed crowd, which was watching the military parade as a show." And the sequel? "Mixed commissions," often of an atro-

cious character, condemned thousands of innocent men to death, transportation, or exile. Where was then, one may ask, Louis-Napoleon's renowned kindliness? He had written in his *Idées Napoléoniennes:* "The Imperial eagle . . . was never stained with French blood shed by French troops. Few governments can say as much about their flag!" Not he about his own any longer.

The plebiscitarian Caesar "had not grown up with the French aristocracy, the French court, the French army, the French people," writes Mr. Guérard. "He remained on the throne an enigma, an adventurer, an exile." And like Napoleon I he "was saddled with the Bonapartes." One of them, Pierre, son of Lucien, was "a fit subject for a picaresque romance." But Louis-Napoleon himself and his favourite cousin, Napoleon, "in their exalted sphere had in them something of the Pierre Bonaparte element: they too are disquieting, they elude normal classification; they are both Caesars and *déclassés"*; while Morny, an illegitimate son of Napoleon III's mother, and Walewski, a bastard of Napoleon I, both leading Ministers of the Second Empire, were "the perfect models of aristocratic adventurers." Morny was a man of affairs—promoter, speculator, and profiteer *par excellence*—"his secret information and his great influence as a statesman were freely used to foster his private schemes." And he was not the only one of that type in the doubtful *équipe* of the Second Empire, which, says Mr. Guérard, "was free from bourgeois pettiness, but also lacked some of the bourgeois virtues." The view that it was not a régime but a racket is not altogether unfounded.

The gaudy Empire "on its glittering surface . . . was a military régime"; "the great reviews . . . were an essential part of its political strategy"; "the days of

bourgeois drabness were over"; gold
braid and epaulets, much martial display, conspicuous waste and maladmin-
istration. "War was made into a blend
of the circus, the tournament, and the
quest. There was a dash of gaiety about
it all ... the spirit of Cyrano and d'Ar-
tagnan." Louis-Napoleon "believed in
the army, but not in war.... He
believed implicitly that he was born a
soldier ... it was faith without works." ...
"At Magenta ... he was sluggish, almost
paralysed. When Frossard came with
the news: 'Sire, a glorious victory!'
the queer 'victor' could hardly credit
his luck: 'And I was going to order a
retreat!' " "The Empire ... in its war-
like aspect was an imitation, and feeble
at the core." Napoleon III "was unmilitary in his ineradicable gentleness....
A philanthropist at the head of an army
is a pathetic absurdity."

A "philanthropist" and a "policeman": for the army at home was "a vast
police force in reserve," "held in readi-
ness against any possible uprising of the
democratic great cities." "Napoleon III
the Policeman was not in contradiction
with Napoleon III the Socialist"; "racketeer, policeman, reformer . . . were
mingled in that equivocal figure." In
the social reformer, "the romanticist
whose dreams were of the future ... and
translated themselves into terms of en-
gineering," who realized that "modern
industry is collectivistic" and through the
Imperial power wanted to give it a collective sense, Mr. Guérard tries to find
atonement for Napoleon III's failure in
all other spheres. Still, the éloge is hardly
convincing; Napoleon III talked the humanitarian jargon of his generation and
shared its mechanic interests and hob-
bies, but no convincing evidence is ad-
duced of original ideas or personal
achievements. And, intermixed with vast

unproven claims, appears the admission
that his economic and social policies
"are no less perplexing than his manage-
ment of foreign affairs"—which is saying a great deal.

For Napoleon III's foreign policy was
shallow and utterly confused. He believed in peace and was out to tear up
the Treaty of Vienna; he believed in
nationality and claimed for France her
"natural frontiers"; he wanted Italy free
but not united; in eighteen years he
waged three major European wars and
sent three expeditions overseas, without
ever seeming to know what he was after.
At first luck covered up, to some extent,
his muddles and blunders. But after
1860 "the series of setbacks, wrong
guesses, false moves on the part of the
Government was unbroken." ... There
was perplexity, aimless drift, and obscure
dismay. By 1867 French hegemony was
at an end; France felt "intolerably hu-
miliated," the Emperor was "infinitely
weary." ...

But here is a last attempt at justification: "Everywhere," writes Mr. Guérard,
"in Paris, in provincial France, in Algeria, the true monuments of the Second
Empire are its public works." (Faust,
who sold his soul for power, concludes
his life over "public works.") "The transformation of Paris, his personal conception ... was so nobly conceived that after
half a century it was still adequate." The
pulling down and rebuilding of capitals
is again a recurrent feature in the history
of despots and dictators, from Nero to
Mussolini and Hitler. Self-expression,
glorification, and commemoration are
one motive. But there is also a deeper,
unconscious urge, born of fear; of things
lurking in the dark, narrow streets of
old cities, the product of organic, un-
controlled growth.... With Napoleon
III such fears found a conscious ra-

tionalization: open spaces were needed for a "whiff of grapeshot." But when his empire fell not one shot was fired.

The careers of Napoleon III and Hitler have shown how far even a bare minimum of ideas and resources, when backed by a nation's reminiscences or passions, can carry a man in the political desert of "direct democracy"; and the books written about Napoleon III, show how loath posterity is to accept the stark truth about such a man. And yet a careful examination of the evidence merely confirms the opinion of leading contemporaries about him: the enigma was not so much in him as in the disparity between his own spiritual weight and that of the ideas centred on him. Dream pictures are best projected on to a blank screen—which, however, neither fixes nor brings them to life.

How much can be safely said of Napoleon III? Biographers agree that there was something in him which defies definition and description: obviously the unstable, the shapeless, the void cannot be delineated. He was reticent, secretive, conspiratorial; at times his "power of silence" created the appearances of strength. Narrow and rigid in his ideas, out of touch with reality, he was a dreamer entertaining vast, nebulous schemes, but vacillating, confused, and therefore complex and ineffective in action. There was in him a streak of vulgarity. He was sensual, dissolute, undiscriminating in his love-affairs: his escapades were a form of escapism, a release. He was benign, sensitive, impressionable, suggestible, yet "gently obstinate." He talked high and vague idealism, uncorrelated to his actions. He had a fixed, superstitious, childish belief in his name and star. Risen to power, this immature weak man became a public danger. His

silence was self-defence: to cover up his inadequacy and to preserve him from the impact of stronger personalities, of demands which he would have found difficult to resist, of arguments to which he had no reply; it also helped him to avoid commitments. . . . He tumbled into situations, neither designed nor deliberately created by him. When forced to act, the day-dreamer would try to draw back: so it was before the *coup d'État,* and again in 1859—in fact in almost every crisis. . . .

With all the pretence to destiny, he was personally modest, for he himself was anonymous under his great name. . . . "Quand on porte notre nom" is a recurrent phrase in his letters to Prince Napoleon; but in one, written some time in 1848, he thus expostulates with his cousin:

you have sense and tact, and you ought to realize that it is hardly suitable for you to sign yourself publicly Napoleon Bonaparte, without any other Christian name, for you to sign yourself like the Emperor, with nothing to distinguish you. And no one seeing your signature knows who it is. I always have myself called Louis-Napoleon, to distinguish me from my relatives. I wish I could call myself Louis-Napoleon Nabuchodonosor Bonaparte in order better to mark my identity [*afin d'avoir une personification bien marquée*]. . . . To sign Napoleon Bonaparte looks unspeakably pretentious—that's all. . . .

Two things emerge clearly: Louis-Napoleon's annoyance at his cousin's identifying himself with the Emperor, and the consciousness of himself being in danger of losing his own identity in such an identification. And indeed as Emperor he was like an actor surrendering his own personality. He became a screen for memories and dreams, with the caption: Napoleon,

OCTAVE AUBRY (1881–1946) was a talented author who wrote extensively on Napoleonic subjects, including biographies of Napoleon, the King of Rome, and Eugenie. In his book *The Second Empire*, which has been widely read, he is favorable to the emperor without being overly sentimental. This excerpt is Aubry's sympathetic summing up of the Second Empire and Napoleon III. His interpretation of Napoleon III's moral leadership contrasts with such views as Namier's; he minimizes the emperor's role as a national leader and credits him with real stature as a great European.*

► *The Second Empire*

As long as the consequences of the catastrophe of 1870 weighed in all their enormity upon France, it was hardly possible for any Frenchman to consider the period of the Second Empire and its major actors with any of the dispassionateness that scientific history requires. A half century had to go by, the Treaty of Versailles had to erase the Treaty of Frankfort, before even a little restraint could influence a thinking that had all along been distorted by too much rancour. The World War, with its bleeding, dripping hands, finally thrust the War of 1870 into history and removed it from the clash of partisan opinion.

Then at least it became possible to view Napoleon III and his reign with the detachment which alone enables the historian to see the true meaning of things that are no more.

The Second Empire was a most extraordinary experiment in revival and imitation. Napoleon III was a more or less genuine nephew of the Corsican. But he was closer to the first Napoleon in spirit than he was in family relationship. As a disciple smitten with admiring wonder, Napoleon III tried, during all the ascending period of his curve, to make that curve coincide exactly with the orbit followed by the victor of Austerlitz.

* Translated by Arthur Livingston and reprinted from Octave Aubry, *The Second Empire* (Philadelphia: J. B. Lippincott Company, 1952). Used by permission of Librairie Arthème Fayard, publishers of the original work, *Le Second Empire* (Paris, 1938).

The 2nd of December was, or could be supposed to be, the 18th of Brumaire. The Presidency tried to suggest the Consulate. Napoleon III also had his war with Italy. But at this point the parallelism which he had sought so deliberately got control of him and strangled him. The war in Mexico was the war in Spain, the war with Prussia was the war with Russia. Sedan was Waterloo. Contemporaries could hardly perceive such relationships in the beginning. Napoleon III and Persigny were the only ones to be more or less instinctively conscious of it. Changed times and exteriors, changed people, timbered the Second Empire with sentiments, interests, theories, facts, which were original and which the First had not known.

Louis Napoleon had in his favor the same extraordinary luck that did so much for Napoleon Bonaparte. He went as far as the latter went. Then his luck changed. Nothing any longer seemed to work—which was a way of saying that the mistakes that had been committed during the early period of the reign combined into one mass of influences to overwhelm it in its latter days.

When he set out to restore the Empire the son of Hortense was thinking not merely of finding a crown for himself and good places in life for the hungry and eager camarilla about him. He also wanted to wipe out the defeat that revolutionary and imperial France had suffered at Waterloo. He wanted to rebuild Europe according to the desires or interests of the peoples, not according to the desires or interests of the kings. That was no mean outlook. It had scope and it had its nobility. It was in accord with the general drift of feeling in France. Napoleon III had some success at first. If he failed in the end it was for a complex of reasons that are not all at-tributable to him, that depend partly on circumstances and partly on the qualities of the people with whom he had to deal. His basic mistake comes down to the fact that he was not able to make the right choices of assistants at the right times in either his domestic or his foreign policy.

Bonaparte issued from the 18th of Brumaire with his hands unsoiled. Napoleon III won his dictatorship by a bloody act of force. This was less his fault than the fault of Morny, but he had to bear the responsibility for it. After such a *coup d'état* no way was left open except arbitrary rule. In a country like France, situated in a modern world, a system so dictatorial had little chance of lasting. Sooner or later the turn towards liberty had to be taken. Memories of the 2nd of December and the whole chain of people and habits that the 2nd of December dragged along in its wake prevented the Empire from taking that turn at the right moment, the moment, that is, when the imperial system was still strong and brilliant and when concessions that it wanted to make and eventually had to make could be made without seeming to be conquests wrenched from a tottering dynasty.

In the regard of Europe, however set the Emperor may have been on his principle of nationalities, he showed backslidings in plenty towards the traditional policy of France—a wise and sound policy—of maintaining a balance of power in Europe and of protecting the independence of small states. Each of the two policies had plenty in its favor. Napoleon III should have adopted the one or the other frankly. The attempt to combine them gave rise to an altogether incoherent, an altogether chaotic diplomacy. Prosecuted in the deepest dark with sudden, startling emergencies, Napoleon III's hybrid policy aroused mistrust and hostility in other countries and brought France to a humiliation that had had no parallel since the Hundred Years' War.

Too many ideas were stirring around in the head of the second Emperor. They were noble, broadminded ideas most often, but the attempt to reconcile them the one with the other raised unsolvable problems. How could France, how could the other countries, long retain faith in this juggler of antimonies? He called himself a child of the Revolution but also a child of the Church. He wanted peace but he also wanted France to have her "natural" frontiers. He stood forth as the mandatory of the people but be insisted on keeping absolute authority. He was well aware of the incompatibilities. Since he could not harmonize them, he disguised them, compromised, played for time.

From the point of view of politics pure and simple, the reign of Napoleon III could only look like a reign of uncertainty and compromise. It was based on principles that sooner or later it had to repudiate or else ignore: peace, the Church, the alliance with England, the army. He abandoned all these foundations one after the other, fighting a series of needless wars, sacrificing the Papacy to Italian unity, flouting English good will, letting his military establishment go to rack and ruin. What wonder then that he was unsteady on his legs and finally fell? Governments can have no ethical principles that are very definite. They must have practical principles and they must adhere to them on peril of their lives.

There were fields in which Napoleon III's ideas were clearer and more coherent and in which they yielded indisputably happy results—the economic

and social fields, for instance. Napoleon III was an out-and-out urbanist. He rioted in public works, demolishing and rebuilding cities and towns to adapt them to modern needs. He invented credit in its modern form and therefore made wealth more flexible and increased it. He tried to increase production by increasing mechanization, meantime lowering the cost of living by free trade. Much of his thought was devoted to the poorer classes. He favored raises in wages and better laboring conditions. He increased as far as he could the numbers of institutions relating to relief and involving group activities.

This phase of his life makes him a great prince, one of the most constructive that have ruled in Europe. In very truth he was the first modern monarch, applying his power to progress. One may safely say that France has never known such contented years. At its high point, around 1860, the Second Empire took the form of a nationalism that had a social outlook, without bearing any resemblance to what is commonly known today as a totalitarian system. Private property was solidly established. Taxes were low. Power favored concentrations of capital but always kept a practical and intelligent eye on the interests of the world of labor.

These are not the only merits of the Second Empire. It rescued the country from the disorderly demagogueries of 1848. It established peace in the field of religion, restoring the Church to a prestige which it had never enjoyed since the heyday of the old monarchy. During the Second Empire France again, over a period of ten years, held leadership in Europe. From the treaty of Paris down to Sadowa France was the preponderant influence in European affairs.

This enviable and in fact envied position Napoleon III owed to the alliance with England and the Crimean War. The latter was too costly an enterprise, but in the light of its consequences it could be justified. The real mistakes came afterwards. The war in Italy upset French policy and drove it out of the world of realities into the world of ideologies. It seems, to be sure, that considering Napoleon III's past and the balance of the various currents of opinion in France, the Italian war was really unavoidable; but in that case it could have been better utilized by adopting a clear-cut attitude at the very beginning and by foreseeing the consequences and accepting them. By conspiring with Cavour, by making promises he could not keep, by allowing the Roman Question to develop into an incurable cancer, the Emperor lost the Italians, the Pope and his Catholics to boot. To be sure he got Nice and Savoy, but that very fact tended to intensify his dependence on his interests in Italy, which thereafter was to become one of his main preoccupations and in almost every crisis to cloud his judgment.

Mexico was a deplorable adventure from first to last. Even had it proved successful it could have ended in no real or considerable profit to France. Possibly too much stress has been laid upon the Mexican blunder. The expedition, taken in its accurate proportions, was very small business. Its worst effects lay in its weakening of the Empire's prestige in public opinion at home. Whatever may have been said on the point, Mexico had nothing to do with the Empire's fatal inactivity during the Austro-Prussian War of 1866.

His policy towards that conflict was the capital and fatal mistake of Napoleon III. He had two courses open to him: either he could have allowed Ger-

many to achieve her national unity around a nucleus, Prussia—and this would have been wholly in line with the nationality principle of which he was the outstanding promoter; or he could have resisted German unification and sided with Austria in order not to have too powerful a rival on his Rhine flank. Once again he proved unable to make his choice. Bismarck stood ready to talk business. Instead of talking business Napoleon III ran off and hid in the clouds, so allowing a crisis to develop for which he had not in the least prepared the country. Physically ill, his mental energy greatly impaired, he allowed himself to drift along on the surface of events. He looked on while Bismarck crushed Austria. Then when the Chancellor no longer feared him, he pressed annoying demands for compensations at the expense of small and friendly countries. Very little was left to French prestige after that.

With the danger from Prussia growing Napoleon III really tried to reorganize his army; but even when he still had the power to do so, he failed to force his will upon an inferior parliament. Then when he had a disorganized army, no generals and no allies at all, he joined in the public clamor instead of moderating it and so walked blindly into the trap that Bismarck had set for him.

When he was conquered, overwhelmed by a frightful disaster, he did his country one last bad turn and the worst, the one that was most damaging to the country's future. When he handed his sword to the King of Prussia at Sedan he could have made peace. Bismarck offered him peace, and the terms he would have insisted on would have been much less onerous than the terms that were to be forced five months later upon the Government of National Defense.

At that moment Napoleon III should have sacrificed his name and his dynastic pride to his country's interests. He preferred to step down before the Regency, knowing well that the Regency could not last a week. Having led France into the quagmire, he should have tried to extricate her at the least possible cost. He would certainly have been overthrown afterwards, but France would not have been so badly cut up—she would not have borne him such a bitter grudge for so long a time.

That Napoleon III had his faults cannot therefore be denied. They are many and great. To be sure he was a man of his time and many errors, many blindspots, that most people of his time had he was bound to have. He simply threw them into relief by his acts, giving them force and conspicuous expression.

His worst stroke of bad luck, if we except the too early collapse of his physical health, was the fact that in his counsel as well as in the army he happened to encounter few if any exceptional abilities, men who were capable of really working with him and preventing him from adopting the unwise course when he was headed in a wrong direction. He was able to work out his counterfeit of the other Empire only on a very secondary plane in this respect. Genius there was none and even talent was scarce. Brains were small, characters very ordinary. Morny was the best of them all, but he could hardly be compared with his grandfather, Talleyrand. Rouher was an efficient administrator, but what was he beside a Cambacérès? Who was Napoleon III's Fouché? Certainly not Maupas, certainly not Pietri. Consider Bonaparte's marshals—Murat, Ney, Lannes, Davout, Masséna, Berthier; and then balance them against the captains of the Second Empire—the best that can be found: Saint-Arnaud, Canrobert, Niel, MacMahon! The only real general that Napoleon III met was probably Pélissier—and Pélissier vanished from the scene in 1864.

The most interesting, at bottom, of all the men of the period, the man who seems really superior in spite of weaknesses and deficiencies, is always Napoleon III himself. Where others saw the big adventure he saw the mission, and he had a blind faith in the mission, in the need of it, in the good it would do. That lifts him at the outset somewhat above the mere political gambler who plays a risky game with his eye strictly on the stakes. He none the less staked his throne too far and trusted too much in his star. He can be condemned since he did not win—success is the one criterion for judging a statesman. But his distinctiveness as a "reform sovereign" cannot be disputed. The liberal Empire, the last product of his system, was an experiment that is worthy of the closest attention and respect. This death-bed marriage of dictatorship and liberty might have proved more satisfactory, perhaps, than the limited monarchy of Louis Philippe, though this last was certainly preferable on a number of other grounds, on the grounds, namely, that it had a principle and a tradition and was basically pacific and did not like adventures. The liberal Empire, as Napoleon III finally worked it out, was well suited to a people that has its liking for strong government but at the same time wants a certain amount of elbow-room—the room required, for instance, for talking, which in France is a real need though no one pays any great attention to what is said. The liberal Empire would have been not a military dictatorship but a people's rights monarchy, pretty to look at and possessing flexible institutions that could readily have been improved.

From a broader point of view one can only be impressed with the important rôle that Napoleon III played in rearing the structure of modern Europe. Whether or not his policies were wholly to the interest of France, he contributed very substantially to the rise of two of the great modern nations—Germany and Italy. He favored the one, he actively helped the other. He dreamed of freeing Poland and had his reign lasted a little longer he would probably some day have gone to war in her behalf. Italy owes Napoleon III quite as much as she owes Victor Emmanuel or Cavour. She has done her best to forget the debt, but had it not been for the second Emperor Italy would have had to suffer a much longer time before winning her rightful place in our present-day world.

Rarely were Napoleon III's ideas selfish or narrowminded, and the fact is probably due to his early life and education. Quite as often as not he reasoned less like the head of a particular state than like a citizen of a larger Europe. "In this whole business," grumbled Thiers in 1866, "I can see that now we are Italians and now we are Germans. I cannot see that we are ever Frenchmen."

The rebuke was not without foundation. Napoleon III was deeply concerned with the interests of the French nation, but he thought they could be reconciled with the broader interests of the Continent. He thought the day would come when a higher court of reference would pass on differences between peoples and end wars. To hasten the advent of that rational era he tried to instill Europe with the habit of going into conference.

As the years roll by this particular significance of the career of Napoleon III will be better and better appreciated. It is within the range of possibility that, when the day of a truly impartial history dawns, he may be ranked higher, much higher, than his contemporary, Bismarck. Bismarck was just a great German. He succeeded on a national plane but by brutally destroying the European spirit.

"There's no Europe left now," said Beust after Sedan.

Beust was more than right. Europe, Europe, that is, as a complex of common ways of feeling, thinking, and doing, of mutual goodwill and understanding, of friendship in a word, came to an end in 1870. The sense of oneness among the European countries had been latent but effective. After Bismarck those countries were to shut themselves up inside aggressive nationalisms that were to lead to the murderous follies of 1914. From them one may wonder whether Western civilization is ever to rise again.

Now through mistakes of his own, now through bad luck, the bearing of which upon his career should never be minimized, Napoleon III may not have brought his strictly French task to full completion—though even in this regard he can claim very considerable merits. He never ceased to be a great European. History will recognize this fact, the history, that is, which recovers the lines that endure from the flux of varying fact. History undoubtedly will look at Napoleon III as one of the forerunners, one of those forerunners whom fate betrays in their attempt to realize great conceptions.

A respected authority on nineteenth- and twentieth-century French history, GORDON WRIGHT (1912–) presents an analysis of the Second Empire that is unusually perceptive and well-balanced. He is able to take note of the problem of authoritarianism and neurotic fear of the strong man that has so colored later political life in France without making a Hitler out of Napoleon III. Although his evaluation of Napoleon III is generally unfavorable, the emperor emerges as an extremely complex subject. This approach gives the narrative an air of objectivity missing in the selections by Namier and Aubry.*

The Imperial Experiment, 1852–1870

Only twice in the century and a half since 1815 has parliamentary or quasi-parliamentary government in France been interrupted by frankly authoritarian systems. These two exceptions, the Second Empire and the Vichy regime, both appear to be aberrations from the country's norm, and both were generally denounced as such after their overthrow. In the case of the Second Empire, however, the passage of time eventually brought a revisionist current and suggested to many Frenchmen that there had been unsuspected virtues in Napoleon III's system. Some biographers converted the emperor from an unscrupulous tyrant into an almost visionary reformer and patron of progress. Many economists pointed out that the period of the Second Empire brought the most rapid economic and social change in French history, and that it strikes the retrospective observer as a kind of watershed between the France of the old regime and the France of the twentieth century. Some historians even suggested that Napoleon's system came nearer than any other to reconciling the diverse traditions—libertarian, equalitarian, authoritarian—left to posterity by the Great Revolution. The new legend has doubtless been exaggerated in some respects, but it does permit a more balanced view than was possible in the years after Napoleon's fall.

Built into the empire were a number

of inconsistencies that have always made it difficult to analyze. The regime's emphasis on glory stood in at least potential contrast to Napoleon's enduring interest in the right of nationalities to self-determination. Its stress on the defense of order and stability seemed incompatible with Napoleon's encouragement of dynamic change. Its authoritarian beginnings are hard to reconcile with its gradual liberalization, a process that eventually turned it into a quasi-parliamentary system resembling that of 1814-48. Perhaps these inconsistencies prove that the imperial regime was nothing more than a haphazard jumble, reflecting the confused welter of ideas within the opportunistic emperor's mind, and prevented by its very nature from arriving at any sort of harmonious fusion. But an even more persuasive hypothesis is that Napoleon, a man of complex and imaginative temperament, sensed some of the trends of his times and sought, in quite un-Cartesian fashion, to adapt an old and complex nation to those trends. If his course was sometimes illogical and his system hybrid, it can only be said that perfect symmetry and logic have not always been the hallmarks of durable systems.

The Second Empire divides itself into two major periods: the authoritarian phase to 1859, the liberal phase thereafter. The transition from one to the other was closely linked with a change in foreign policy that sharply affected Napoleon's relations with the church, and a change in tariff policy that affected his relations with the business group. . . . Napoleon's turn toward domestic liberalization that began late in 1859 and continued jerkily throughout the next decade may have been merely an attempt to find a new base of support in place of that lost through his foreign and

economic policies. Perhaps the emperor and his advisers slipped into this dangerous current under pressure of circumstances, through mere opportunism or sheer weakness, somewhat against their own preferences and without any clear idea of where the current might carry them. But it is equally possible that the evolution of the 1860's was both planned and desired; that it had been, from the very outset of the empire, the more or less conscious intention of Napoleon and of certain advisers like Morny; that it was the product of an ambition to reconcile the conflicting political traditions inherited from France's past. A choice between these interpretations depends on an estimate of motives and therefore permits no sure or easy answer. But a second problem is equally crucial. Whatever the motivation of Napoleon and his entourage may have been, was their new course after 1859 a sensible and realistic one? Was it, by 1870, on the way to producing a viable compromise system of government, or was it dragging the regime into a morass of hopeless contradictions? Was this kind of authoritarian system capable of mellowing without destroying itself? Here again, no easy or certain answer is possible; yet some answer must be attempted if the record of the empire is to be judged as well as narrated.

The political system of the authoritarian phase requires only brief analysis. Its institutions were frankly borrowed from those of the First Empire: the façade of legislative organs without much prestige or power, the ministry responsible to the emperor alone, the plebiscite as an occasional device to give the illusion of popular control. Napoleon justified this attempt to resurrect the past by remarking that for fifty years France had retained the administrative, judicial, religious, and financial structure established by Napoleon I, so that a return to his political institutions was only logical and consistent. In a relatively mild sense, the new empire was a police state. Opposition to the regime was possible, but it was narrowly restricted by controls on the press and on the right to hold public meetings. The modern concentration camp did not yet exist, but there was its primitive equivalent in the penal colonies of Guiana and Algeria. Most of the regime's outspoken critics had chosen exile in preference to prison or deportation: among them were such notables as Thiers, Victor Hugo, and Louis Blanc. Silent but bitter antagonism persisted among diehard republicans, Legitimist aristocrats, and most Orleanist politicians, though some Orleanists were converted by Napoleon's policy of aid to enterprising business men.

Support for the regime during its authoritarian decade came not only from the business class but also from the church hierarchy, from the bulk of the peasantry, and from a considerable minority of the urban workers. Churchmen knew that Napoleon was a freethinker, but they applauded his support of the Pope's temporal power and his defense of social order; some bishops heaped on their adulation with a trowel, publicly comparing the emperor to Constantine and Saint Louis. Napoleon's proletarian support came from those workers who were embittered and disillusioned with the republicans after 1848. Bonapartist candidates who promised vigorous measures of economic expansion caught the fancy of at least some working-class elements, and the boom of the 1850's kept them relatively content. The peasants, save for those few

who voted red or the larger number who remained subservient to local aristocrats, contributed the regime's mass base. Many of them were moved by considerations of glamor and glory, many by a conviction that Napoleon would repress radicals and *partageux*. But there were some who clearly betrayed quite opposite motives—who voted for Bonapartist candidates as a kind of declaration of independence from the local notables who had dominated them for so long. At least the beginnings of peasant education in the use of the ballot can be traced to the era of the Second Republic and the Second Empire; as early as 1849 peasant voters in certain regions had shaken off the docility that marked their voting behavior in April, 1848, and had turned to republican or Bonapartist candidates. This rebellious sense of independence benefited Bonapartism in the early years, but in the long run it was to undermine the regime's support in the countryside. Once a stiff-necked peasant had learned that he could safely ignore the admonitions of the local aristocrat, priest, or notary, he was likely to rebel against the pressures of Napoleon's prefects as well.

The authoritarian empire left only a restricted sphere for active political life. Sessions of the Corps Législatif (the new lower house of parliament) were closed to the public, and only a brief summary of its proceedings was made available in the press. Although the Corps was elected by universal manhood suffrage, Napoleon was careful to space the elections at intervals of six years. "I am prepared to be baptized with the water of universal suffrage," he is supposed to have said, "but I don't intend to live with my feet in a puddle." The plebiscite, a device theoretically designed to indicate the responsibility of the emperor to the people, was actually used only three times: in 1851, 1852, and 1870.

Yet it would be unjust to conclude that the authoritarian empire anticipated the totalitarian system of Hitler, or that the empire was run by a hand-picked collection of Bonapartist fanatics and puppets. In creating the new political class whose function it was to shore up and administer the empire, Napoleon and his advisers did not confine themselves to "pure" Bonapartists, nor did they seek to sweep away the old elites in favor of a new privileged caste. Instead, they drew heavily on the existing elites, in an effort to combine aristocracy with democracy. "Official candidates" for the Corps Législatif—i.e., those who were actively patronized by the government—were not hand-picked in Paris but were often selected by the imperial prefects from among the local notables whose influence might get them elected and whose support (if it could be won) would be valuable to the regime. Although many of the notables resisted the government's blandishments and remained loyal to a previous regime, a fair number of ex-Legitimists and ex-Orleanists gradually let themselves be converted. The effect was to shunt aside many of the early Bonapartists of more modest social origins who had rallied to Louis Napoleon's cause in 1848 and had begun to build local party machinery. The Second Empire thus came to be a curious alliance of old and new forces, and it represented neither a total break with France's political past nor a revolutionary change in the locus of power within French society. The lower middle class, so heavily represented in the political elite of twentieth-century fascist states, got little satisfaction out of Napoleon III's revolution. Not until the middle years of the Third Republic did this

segment of society work its way up into the controlling circles of the state.

Napoleon's ministers and high administrative offiicals also represented a mixture of old and new. Some, like Persigny, were personal henchmen whose loyalty had been tested in the early days of adversity. Some, like the Duc de Morny and Comte Walewski, were kinsmen of the emperor—illegitimate ones, it is true, but kinsmen nevertheless. Some, like Achille Fould, came from powerful banking families. Some, like Eugène Rouher, Jules Baroche, and Michel Chevalier, were ex-Orleanist lawyers, politicians, or intellectuals. Some, like the prefect Haussmann who rebuilt Paris in its modern form, were career bureaucrats who had served both the monarchy and the republic. Critics of the regime alleged that it was run by a band of shady and unscrupulous adventurers whose qualities reflected the shoddy artificiality of the system. There were men around Napoleon who did fit that description; but the empire had a broader and more reputable base than its enemies' charges would suggest. If the regime was not served by all the elites, that was not because the emperor preferred adventurers to solid citizens, but rather because so many prominent Frenchmen remained irreconcilable after 1851.

Napoleon's first steps toward softening the authoritarian system in 1859 were relatively hesitant ones. Political exiles were amnestied and allowed to return; the Corps Législatif was given the right to present an annual "address" or set formal resolutions to the emperor, and its sessions were opened to the public. More important, however, was the fact that additional reforms followed at irregular intervals throughout the decade. In 1867 Napoleon restored freedom of the press and of political assemblage and granted parliament the right to inter-pellate the ministers. Meanwhile he had given the workers the right to form trade unions and to strike and had ap-proved a significant program of broad-ening public education, drafted by his aggressive minister of education, Victor Duruy. The whole process reached a startling culmination on New Year's Day in 1870, when Napoleon decreed the establishment of a quasi-parliament-ary system. The cabinet was henceforth to be a homogeneous body, responsible to the Corps Législatif and subject to overthrow by it. To indicate his sin-cerity, the emperor chose as prime min-ister Émile Ollivier, a moderate repub-lican who had been a leading figure in opposition circles for a decade. Ollivier was permitted to staff his cabinet with ex-republicans and ex-Orleanists, most of whom had long been exponents of parliamentary government. True, the revised system contained a serious am-biguity: it provided no solution in case there should be a deadlock between emperor and parliament. But a similar ambiguity had existed from 1814 to 1848 and had not prevented a gradual evolu-tion toward something very much like a parliamentary monarchy.

This jerky progress toward "liberal-ized authoritarianism" during the 1860's cost Napoleon much of his conservative support, yet failed to win him enough new friends on the left to counter-bal-ance the loss. Instead, the opposition steadily gained strength at each legis-lative election. . . . On the face of things, it would seem that the emperor's liberal gamble had failed, and that he might have been wiser to revert to a purer form of authoritarianism, buttressed by the support of the church and the business group. Some of his advisers (Persigny,

for example) had so argued all along, and they fought a steady rear-guard ac-tion to check the liberal trend before it was too late.

But though the empire's downfall seems to justify Persigny's warnings, it would be risky to conclude that Napo-leon destroyed himself by attempting to graft liberalism onto an authoritarian root. Those critics who prophesied dis-aster offered no real alternative except stand-pattism—a policy that has rarely succeeded for very long in any modern and dynamic nation. Successful regimes have ordinarily been the ones with enough flexibility to adapt themselves to changing economic, social and psycho-logical conditions. It may be that Na-poleon's reforms were not intelligently conceived, or that he lacked a sense of timing and a knack for public rela-tions and thus lost the benefit that should have accrued from his concessions. At any rate, it does seem certain that after 1859 Napoleon was moving in the right direction so far as the bulk of French opinion was concerned. There can be little doubt that by the end of the decade most Frenchmen favored the establishment of some kind of parlia-mentary system, whether labelled mon-archy, republic, or empire.

There is an apparent contradiction here. If Napoleon was moving in the right direction to satisfy Frenchmen, why did the opposition grow steadily larger and more obstreperous? Partly, no doubt, because greater freedom made it safer to indulge in the pleasures of vocal opposition, so long denied to an assertive people. Still more, perhaps, because many Frenchmen were not satisfied with piecemeal reforms and felt that only a powerful opposition movement could push the emperor all the way to a full-scale parliamentary system. The purpose of much of the opposition in the later 1860's was not to overthrow the dynasty but rather to speed the process of liberalizing the empire; many monarchists, many republicans were prepared to leave Napoleon III in office if he would only accept the principle of responsible government.

The most effective support for this interpretation is offered by the outcome of Napoleon's plebiscite of May, 1870. The emperor had just taken, on New Year's Day, his longest step toward a full-fledged parliamentary regime; and he called on the voters to approve or repudiate that reform. The opposition vote, which had climbed to three and a half million in 1869, plummeted to one and a half million; the progovernment vote rose from four and a half to seven and a half million. No greater victory had been won by the regime since the days of the authoritarian empire. Even though the persistent hard core of opposition was still disturbingly large, it seemed clear that Napoleon had at last found a formula satisfactory to the bulk of the nation.... The record of the liberal decade thus suggests that Napoleon III did grope his way toward a workable governmental system: a system lacking in inner logic, yet potentially capable of reconciling and balancing the nation's most important conflicts.

One crucial question remains, however: Was Napoleon III capable of heading that kind of regime? A compromise system that lacks inner logic, that combines Caesarism and responsible government, calls for exceptionally shrewd, adaptable, pragmatic leadership. The flaws in Napoleon's character make it doubtful that he could have furnished that kind of adept yet vigorous statesmanship. His intimates knew that he had an indolent streak, that he was in-

clined to vacillate, that he indulged at times in wishful thinking in preference to facing hard facts. "Napoleon the Well-Meaning," someone sarcastically called him. If there had been time to try the new experiment in quasi-parliamentary government, Napoleon might have been confronted quite soon with a major challenge to his personal authority; for many of his new supporters were determined to complete the process of liberalization by converting the emperor into a British-type monarch, subordinate to parliament's wishes. No one can be sure that Napoleon would have been flexible enough to take that final logical step in a process that he himself had voluntarily begun....

Events were not to permit the testing of the new hybrid regime; only five months after the triumphant plebiscite, it had collapsed, and the emperor was on his way to exile in England. What doomed the empire was not its internal evolution but rather the cumulative results of a series of errors in foreign policy. By 1870 France found itself isolated and confronted by a powerful new rival across the Rhine. Napoleon had failed to intervene in central Europe in 1866 when it might have been easy to check the growth of Prussian power. He had failed in his subsequent efforts to secure face-saving compensations in the form of territorial gains along the Rhine. He had failed once more when he sought to bolster French military power by introducing a new army bill into parliament in 1867. His proposal, which would have brought a larger annual contingent of draftees into the army and would have increased the cost of preparedness, aroused a political storm; in the end the bill had to be so watered down that it became innocuous. Meanwhile the failure of Napoleon's "great idea"—the building of a Catholic empire in Mexico allied with France—had divided the nation and provided his critics with effective ammunition. . . .

War with Prussia was not the only possible outcome of the crisis that erupted suddenly in July, 1870. Either Bismarck or Napoleon III could have averted a test of arms. Bismarck had no desire to avert it; Napoleon lacked the foresight to do so. Chronic illness during the last years of his reign probably lessened his capacity to devote sustained attention to the developing crisis or to make difficult decisions; he was unwise enough to let authority slip into the hands of his second-rate foreign minister, Gramont. The French government, aroused at the news that Spain had secretly arranged to place a Hohenzollern prince on the Spanish throne, put such heavy pressure on the king of Prussia that the latter persuaded the Hohenzollern nominee to withdraw his candidacy. Gramont had thus won a notable diplomatic victory, but he was not intelligent enough to be satisfied with it. Instead, he demanded still further Prussian assurances for the future, and thus gave Bismarck an opportunity to play the picador to "the Gallic bull." On July 19 the French government, angered at Prussia's flouting of French demands, slipped into war—unnecessarily, unwisely, and with inadequate preparation for so severe a test.

Few Frenchmen except Adolphe Thiers (who had been issuing gloomy warnings ever since 1866) fully understood the threat that France faced. Prime Minister Ollivier encouraged the nation's illusions by announcing that he accepted war "with a light heart," and his war minister even more recklessly assured parliament that the army was ready "to the last gaiter button." What the army

lacked in 1870 was not gaiter buttons but something far more serious: efficient, vigorous, and imaginative leadership. The officer corps, though honorable and loyal, had slipped into a rut of routine-mindedness and smug complacency that contrasted sharply with the tough and keen mentality of the Prussian staff. France's clumsy and antiquated process of mobilization had not even been completed when the first German troops crossed the frontier. Within a month the great border fortress of Metz was cut off by the invaders, and the army of Marshal Bazaine besieged therein. Napoleon, who had gone to the front to share the perils of war with his soldiers, refused to adopt the one strategic plan that might still have averted defeat—a slow retreat to Paris and a stand outside the walls of the capital. Fearing the political repercussions of such a strategic withdrawal, he accompanied his remaining army under MacMahon in an attempt to relieve Metz. The Prussians cornered MacMahon's force at Sedan on August 31 and broke its resistance in a brief battle fought the next day. Napoleon, aware that the fight was hopeless, sought a hero's death in the front lines, on the theory that his martyrdom might save the throne for his adolescent son. Even that consolation was denied him; and he fell ignominiously into the hands of the Prussians.

The emperor, but not the empire, survived the carnage of Sedan. When the news reached Paris on September 3, the regime's political leaders tried desperately to prop up the imperial system by arranging an interim government under a military leader. Even the republican politicians were willing; most of them were not eager to take power at so gloomy a moment. But it was far too late to save the empire; its prestige and glamor had vanished in defeat. On September 4 demonstrating crowds converged on the Corps Législatif and demanded the proclamation of a republic. Napoleon's system disintegrated without bloodshed, and almost without regret.

The Second Empire outlasted any other governmental experiment that had been tried in France since 1814. Whether it achieved more than its predecessors and whether it came nearer to producing a durable compromise are controversial issues. For two generations after its fall the empire was bitterly vilified by all good republicans. Yet by the middle 1870's Bonapartism had revived sufficiently to become an important political force in France; in 1877 there were 104 Bonapartists in the Chamber of Deputies. So quick a recovery (even though it proved fleeting) may suggest that many Frenchmen remembered the days of Napoleon III with nostalgia. Some twentieth-century critics of the parliamentary republic were to find a retrospective utopia in the Second Empire: a middle way, they said, between the divisive weakness of multiparty democracy and the oppressive tyranny of modern totalitarianism. Yet it is quite possible that the consequences of the empire were more destructive than constructive; that this interruption in the nineteenth-century trend toward responsible government created as many problems as it tried to solve, and that some of France's contemporary ailments are at least partly traceable to it. Certainly it deepened the neurotic fear of the strong man among French republicans and liberals and reinforced the sentiment that authority must be both suspected and resisted. After 1870 the new republic was shaped, its institutions were built in an atmosphere of violent revulsion against the Second Empire—even against those aspects of it that might have helped France adapt its political, social, and economic structure to the needs of modern times. . . .

With Napoleon III came the first fundamental change since 1814 in the temper and conduct of French foreign policy. Although Napoleon announced just before the coup d'état of 1851 that "the Empire means peace," no ruler bearing his name was likely to rank peace higher than glory. Nor could any Napoleon fail to regard the treaties of 1815 as a humiliating *Diktat* that must be revised for the sake of national and dynastic prestige. One might think that the task of characterizing the Second Empire's foreign policy would be an easy one; yet quite the contrary is true. Napoleon's conduct of affairs aroused more controversy among contemporaries, and has been more diversely judged by historians, than any other phase in the foreign policy of nineteenth-century France.

To some historians, the emperor was a dreamer hypnotized by the principle of the rights of nationalities; a man whose idealism was not adequately balanced by a sense of realism, and who failed to understand how his dreams might impinge upon the interests of his country. To others, he was a calculating schemer concerned above all with prestige, aiming to dazzle the French people by his exploits, utilizing the nationality principle as a mere pretext to justify his meddling tactics. To still others, he was an admirably farsighted and intelligent statesman who foreshadowed the modern ideals of self-determination and European federation, who wanted France to lead Europe toward that brighter destiny. Finally, there are those who conclude that he had no clear aim at all; they see him as buffeted about by conflicting currents within France and concerned primarily to keep himself in power through shrewd manipulation.

Not only Napoleon's motives, but his alleged errors of judgment as well, have been subjects of continuing controversy. Some critics have charged him with focussing too narrowly on Italian questions, perhaps because his early experiences as a Carbonaro there left a kind of emotional residue. German scholars have accused him, rather, of a persistent determination to recover the Rhine frontier at almost any cost and to keep Germany weak enough to be subservient. Other historians allege that he failed to raise his eyes from the European scene and see that a vast colonial empire could be had for the taking. Still others believe that the emperor's central purpose was to build a great alliance system led by France, and that he bungled the task through his inability to choose among potential allies.

The controversy doubtless stems from Napoleon's complex and contradictory nature and from his habit of secretive, tight-lipped diplomacy. Probably the emperor was neither a rigid doctrinaire, nor an idealistic dreamer, nor an unprincipled opportunist. His interest in the rights of nationalities seems to have been genuine; but almost certainly it was not the core of his policy, the central aim for which he would sacrifice all else. He made no effort, for example, to push that principle in the Balkan region, where it would have interfered with his ambition to arrange an Austrian alliance. A reasonable conclusion might be that his central aim was a very broad and general one: to restore French prestige in Europe and to give his dynasty a solid base. Napoleon's revisionist attitude toward the treaties of 1815 was almost as fundamental as that of the Germans toward Versailles many decades

later. Apparently the emperor had shaped no rigid program but intended to feel his way in pragmatic fashion toward a restoration of national prestige. His primary goal was neither territorial expansion nor European federation, but a balance-of-power system under France's diplomatic leadership.

During his first decade in power Napoleon sought to achieve this end through close collaboration with Britain. To win London to such a policy was probably his principal motive in entering the Crimean War of 1854–56; certainly French interests in the Near East offered no adequate justification for war with Russia. A warm relationship did develop for a time; the period brought the first use of the phrase "entente cordiale." But the entente gradually cooled after 1860 as the result of a series of minor squabbles, in spite of the closer trade relationships made possible by the Chevalier-Cobden Treaty.

As a kind of substitute for the Anglo-French alignment, Napoleon turned to a device that had long attracted him: a revival of the European congress system of the Castlereagh era. The emperor's interest in diplomacy by conference (a practice for which there was little precedent in periods of peace) lends some plausibility to the thesis that he was a kind of European federalist. He conceived of the congress system, however, much as Castlereagh had done— as a mechanism for operating a balance-of-power system.... Simultaneously during these middle years of the empire, Napoleon was embarking on a whole series of enterprises that aroused the suspicions of the rest of Europe and that produced division at home: aid to Piedmont in creating a north Italian federation, intervention in Mexico to carve out a sphere of influence there, an expedition to Syria (1860) with the declared purpose of protecting Christians against Moslem persecution, penetration of Indo-China as a base from which to tap the Chinese market.

From 1866 onward the empire entered a third phase, during which Napoleon was increasingly preoccupied with the German problem. This was not to be the most brilliant phase of Napoleonic diplomacy; indeed, the disaster of 1870 was prepared in considerable part by the mistakes of the prewar years. The emperor seriously underestimated both Prussia's potential power and Bismarck's skill and ruthlessness. He even helped the Prussians get a treaty with Italy in 1866—a treaty that was essential to Bismarck's plans for an armed showdown with Austria. It is quite clear that he expected a standoff fight between Prussia and Austria, with France stepping in at the proper moment to mediate and to dictate terms. A few Frenchmen perceived the danger more clearly: Thiers, for example, who publicly warned the government on May 3, 1866. Napoleon ignored the warning; but even when the battle of Sadowa proved Thiers right, he failed to intervene while there was still time. After some hesitation, he gave up the idea of concentrating an army on the Rhine—probably because most French opinion was so vigorously and vocally hostile to the idea.

The fatal error of inaction in 1866 was compounded during the years that followed. Napoleon's clumsy efforts to get territorial compensation along the Rhine only played into Bismarck's hands. His attempts to negotiate alliances with Italy and Austria dragged on to an empty conclusion; and his desperate attempt to build up France's military power was defeated by an irritated public opinion at home. By the time of the decisive crisis in July, 1870, Napoleon seems to have let the power of decision slip almost entirely out of his hands—the result, at least in part, of chronic illness. It may be that the emperor saw more clearly than either his advisers or his subjects during the last years before his downfall. But even if that was the case, he no longer showed the leadership and the determination required to conduct an unpopular but hardheaded policy. Napoleon's inadequacy as a crisis leader left the nation, at the end of his eighteen-year reign, reduced in prestige, isolated in Europe, and threatened with demotion to the status of a second-rate power. Perhaps that decline was not entirely chargeable to him; perhaps the facts of geography, resources, and population were beginning to catch up with the French. But it would be futile to deny that Napoleon deserved an important share of the blame. Confronted by a rival as able and unscrupulous as Bismarck, the emperor's shortcomings as a shaper of foreign policy could no longer be concealed.

The British historian THEODORE ZELDIN (1933–   ) is a Research Fellow of St. Antony's College at Oxford. Author of several articles and a book, *The Political System of Napoleon III,* he has carefully explored French archives for new information on the social and political structure of France during the Second Empire. He sees the emperor as a responsible conservative politician who was able to work with a number of disparate elements. The present article by Zeldin responds by inference to Namier and Guedalla, as well as to other critics of Napoleon III, and suggests a new context in which the emperor may be viewed.*

► # The Myth of Napoleon III

"Read no history, nothing but biography, for that is life without theory." So Disraeli once said, but it is not a maxim that can be applied to Napoleon III. His life contained so many adventures, conspiracies and love affairs, his court was so well provided with gossip and intrigue, his career reached such depths and such heights of fortune, that it is no wonder that his biographers have not had time to stop to ask what he achieved as a statesman. They would have been surprised to know that he was, in the opinion of Lamartine, the greatest politician France had had since Talleyrand, and possibly even greater than he.

It is not from any personal animosity that they refuse to treat him seriously. On the contrary, for it can be said of few, as it can be said of him, that no one who ever knew him detested him or even found him disagreeable. His gift for making friends was quite extraordinary, and even his bitterest enemies concede that he was an amiable man. That, in fact, is how they damn him. He was a pleasant man, they say, with good intentions, no doubt, but with no political gifts and with none of the ability necessary to carry out his grandiose schemes. He was a rake, an adventurer, a dreamer, a charlatan, but nothing like his uncle, of course.

He ended as he began, in exile, and his critics have enjoyed showing that his failure was inevitable. He gradually di-

---

* From Theodore Zeldin, "The Myth of Napoleon III," *History Today,* February, 1958, by permission of *History Today* and the author.

vested himself of much of his power; and they have assumed that he did so because he was compelled to yield before the growing strength of the opposition, and decided to give up his control of the state in order to retain his throne. His Liberal Empire collapsed after little more than a hundred days; and they have assumed that it was a mere epilogue to his reign and not the consummation of his work. His government did not include the old parliamentary leaders; and they have asserted, therefore, that his supporters were mere nonentities and henchmen. They enjoy quoting the pretty phrase attributed to him: "The Empress is legitimist, my cousin is republican, Morny is Orleanist, I am a socialist: the only Bonapartist is Persigny and he is mad"; and from this they conclude that the Second Empire represented nothing but a jumble of second-hand ideas. Some claim that it was established almost accidentally, under the influence of force and excitement, that it had no real roots in the country, and that its motto should have been not "Liberty, Equality and Fraternity" but that given to it by Marx, "Cavalry, Infantry and Artillery."

It is extraordinary how reputations are made and unmade in history.... [I]t is well known how Napoleon I looked after his own reputation and how he created the legend about himself which made his name into a positive political force. After Waterloo, he became the martyr of St. Helena, whence he preached the gospel of his own glory, proclaiming the excellence of his intentions and encouraging posterity to forget everything in his reign that was not to his credit. His political enemies were in power for a bare fifteen years. Louis Philippe erected monuments to his glory and brought his ashes back to France as those of a national hero. Napoleon III

gave him another twenty years of official worship, published his correspondence in fifty volumes and so made it impossible for anyone ever to deny his greatness. His reputation never had to contend seriously with popular hostility or ignorance.

Exactly the opposite happened to Napoleon III. His martyrdom in the fortress of Ham took place before his reign; and though it helped him to gain his throne, it came too early to influence historical opinion. In 1873 he planned to repeat the return from Elba, but died before he could do so. The literary world was largely hostile to him and vilified him as *Napoléon le petit*. The two best histories of his reign are by a republican and a royalist, and the French school text-books have long reflected the views of his political enemies, who obtained the professorships after his fall. He has, indeed, never been allowed to speak for himself: his published correspondence barely fills a few volumes and most of it dates from his early days of exile. There is nothing resembling the huge series on his uncle to show what he was really like as a ruler.

There has thus grown up a myth about Napoleon III as a sort of counterpart to the legend about Napoleon I. It began with the story that he had been elected president because the royalist politicians thought he would be a tool in their hands, a story that they invented to flatter their own importance. There is, in fact, incontrovertible evidence that they supported him because they saw that he was bound to win; and Thiers, who never erred on the side of modesty, would have stood himself had he thought he had any chance at all. The story that he was allowed to take his seat in parliament in June 1848 because he was considered harmless and an imbecile is also an invention from the same source. Rumours were spread that he could not speak French, that his hobby was rearing eagles in cages, that so conscious was he of his own incompetence that he had opened negotiations of his own accord to secure the return of the legitimist pretender. The politicians who met him, however, quickly saw how wide all this propaganda was of the truth. Montalembert, the leader of the liberal Catholics, was much impressed when he first went to see him in October 1848. "I cannot conceive," he noted in his diary, "where his reputation for incompetence comes from."

It is time, therefore, that the abuse of his enemies should be appreciated in its true light and not accepted as impartial history merely because they happened to be distinguished men. What has been said about him should be put aside and an attempt should be made to study the facts and the primary sources. The man, however, cannot be assessed unless his work is also assessed, and that is why biography without history is not enough for him.

His standing as a statesman must depend to a very considerable extent on the way in which the Liberal Empire is interpreted. Napoleon I claimed in exile that his object had always been to establish liberty, and that the Hundred Days were destined to inaugurate a new era of peace and constitutional monarchy. No one has believed him, and quite rightly, for his character and his career made it impossible for him to accomplish such a metamorphosis. Is it right, however, to dismiss the similar claims of Napoleon III? Was he a liberal only in opposition and a despot as soon as he got the reins of power into his own hands?

In truth, he was probably a determined believer in the merits of neither liberalism nor despotism, but an opportunist above all else. . . . Politics was for him "the application of history." The task of the statesman was to study history and to discover which of the driving forces in the world had passed forever and which would triumph. Success would come to him who judged correctly which way the wind was blowing and trimmed his sails accordingly; to him who always made sure to lead events and not to be dragged by them. He must represent the aspirations of his epoch; and that is why his flattering courtiers pleased him by saying, "Sire, you are the century."

"In the end," he once declared, "it is always public opinion that wins the last victory." He concluded from his study of history, and in particular from his study of the history of England, the most successful of monarchies, that "It is not chance that determines the destinies of nations; it is not an unforeseen accident that overthrows or maintains thrones. There is a general cause that determines events and makes them follow logically from each other. A government can often violate law and even liberty with impunity, but if it does not put itself openly at the head of the great interests of civilization, it can have only an ephemeral existence." He would always seek to give the French what they wanted.

In 1848 he was, to an extraordinary extent, "the man of the century"; and he did not owe his success simply to the attraction of his name. He represented better than anyone else the French peasantry, whose hearts were on the left but whose pockets were on the right, who were fond of being "advanced" in theory but who, in the practical conduct of life, sought only the traditional rewards for their labour—property and social advancement for their children. Similarly, Napoleon was at once conservative and radical, a lover of peace but also a lover of glory, an unbeliever married to a religious wife—a bundle of contradictions, but of the very contradictions that were innate in the great majority of his subjects.

He was the only politician of the time who could be conservative without being retrograde. The proclamation of universal suffrage had cast terror into the old parliamentary leaders, who hastened to modify and limit it as soon as they returned to power. Napoleon alone knew how to place himself at the head of such an electorate, to lead it in the direction he chose and so to prove that it could be a perfectly harmless and conservative force. When he fell in 1870, no one could seriously think of abolishing universal suffrage; and this is not the least of his contributions. . . .

. . . The centralization of Louis XIV and Napoleon I placed immense power in the hands of the government, and without the approval or initiative of its head very little could be done. Napoleon III argued that the details of politics mattered little to the peasants, and that they did not care whether there were one or two parliaments in Paris or none at all. He thought that what really interested them was how to finance improvements in their daily existence, how to build roads to their farms and railways to their markets, how to bring water to their villages and how to establish local schools for their children, and how, on top of all this, to find the money to maintain their hospitals and their almshouses, to repair their churches and to embellish their village halls. The centralization of the country required the peasants to pay taxes for these very purposes, but they had to send their money to Paris and then to beg it back from the government. The government was willing to help

those who helped it. . . .

. . . Napoleon had by far the best organized party in the country, for he had at his disposal the civil service, which now reached the zenith of its prestige and its power. The prefects, enjoying their heyday and reproducing in the provinces the glitter of the imperial court, were not simply administrators but the veritable political leaders of their departments. They gave much time to the task of making converts to Bonapartism, wooing the aristocracy with dinner parties and balls, wooing the bourgeoisie with jobs and favours, wooing above all the masses with the gift and the promise of material benefits. They took the credit for the prosperity that the country enjoyed; and it is largely thanks to them that the Second Empire was afterwards remembered as the good old days when men used to play games with golden coins. . . .

. . . The system of voting was different from that now used in England. The voter was not presented with a list of candidates and asked to place a cross against one of them. Instead, he was required to put in the box a ballot paper which he had to produce himself, bearing the name of his favourite. These ballot papers were generally supplied by the candidates; but the government had the advantage that it sent the ballot paper of the candidate it supported with the card that entitled an elector to vote. The ignorant, therefore, frequently came to vote with their electoral cards and their government ballot papers, which they put in the box as though they were the only ones that could be used. When some poor peasant came to the village hall with a ballot paper that an opposition agent had given him, the mayor presiding over the box would at once spot it.

"Ah!" he would say. "Haven't you got

any other ballot paper apart from that one?"

"Why, yes, Monsieur le Maire."

"Show me."

The elector shows several. The mayor takes the official candidate's and says, "Here, my good man, this is the *good one*; put the others down—." Then the mayor puts it into the box. Or he would say, "Put the ballot paper you've got into your pocket and take this one: this is the *good one*."

Such proceedings took place when the mayor was a paternal figure and the elector a submissive peasant. But sometimes a more arrogant man would march into the voting hall and demand a ballot paper. He is given the official candidate's. He asks for "another one." The mayor says there are no others. The man insists. The mayor gets angry. A row would start and in the end the man would probably be thrown out. Of course, the mayor would receive great sympathy; for was not this desire to vote against his advice a challenge to his authority, a doubt cast upon his knowledge of how administrative business should be transacted? It was for personal reasons, as much as because of their political preferences, that the mayors lost their tempers with organizers of opposition. They looked upon dissent as a personal insult. One mayor, no more pompous than most, thus writes to his prefect: "Yesterday three men travelled over my commune, putting up red posters everywhere in favour of M. Casimir Perier. When I and a gendarme asked them by what right they were putting up notices on the wall of the town hall without my authorization, they replied in an *impertinent* manner, that they had no need of my authorization." This was a slur on his dignity and his rage can be imagined.

The mayors had valuable allies in the schoolmasters, who were likewise agents of the state. Here is a report from one of them to show how they acted: "As secretary of the town hall, entrusted in this capacity with the preparation of all the election documents, I was able to exercise far greater influence on the elections. In conjunction with the village constable, I distributed the ballot papers I received from Monsieur le Préfet to the electors. I strongly supported the candidature of M. Arnaud, the government's candidate. I tried to make the electors understand that we must all without exception consolidate the plans of our august Emperor by a unanimous vote. Despite this, I was compelled to redouble my zeal and energy owing to the fact that some agitators had led astray a large number of electors and particularly twenty electors at a village not far away, who had been earnestly solicited to vote for M. Dupont Delporte and were completely disposed to vote for the latter and in consequence to reject the government's candidate. Having heard this vexatious news, I went to make them see the error into which they had fallen. To prove to them that the government is good, I gave them knowledge of a letter which Monsieur le Maire of the commune had received from Monsieur le Préfet, in which it is said that a new subsidy of 220,000 francs had just been given to the department to be divided between the communes that had suffered in the floods of 1856. In the presence of this testimony of the solicitude of the government, you will be so ungrateful, I told them, as to refuse it your co-operation: and at once they all threw down the ballot papers that had been given to them and came at once to the town hall to vote for M. Arnaud."

In the course of the reign this system gradually disintegrated, and by 1869 it had pretty well collapsed. Napoleon himself hastened its collapse by his own measures. He found it unsatisfactory despite, and even because of, the almost absolute power that it gave him. One day, talking with the duc de Plaisance of his days as president of the republic, he said regretfully, "Ah! Those were the days!" Plaisance said things did not seem to have worsened for him. "You are quite wrong, my dear duke," replied Napoleon. "At that time it was all life and movement around me; today it is silence. I am isolated, I no longer hear anything." He was expected to do everything himself, but inevitably, in practice, he could not. He had to bear all the responsibility, nevertheless, while his ministers wielded their immense power without adequate control from parliament or from each other. Both he and they soon perceived that such checks were desirable, quite apart from any ideological reasons, simply in the interests of more efficient government. . . . He was getting old, moreover; and yet as things stood, all the achievements of the reign hung on the life of one sick man. He must provide for the future and found institutions that would render his work permanent.

Many of his earliest supporters had no wish to continue with the old system either. They may have been docile enough when he emerged clothed in all the prestige that his immense victories at the plebiscites gave him; but now they thought it was time they should share his power. They could no longer win their elections in their constituencies simply by declaring their loyalty to him, by saying, as did an old veteran of Waterloo, "If you re-elect me, I shall, as before, support the Empire and we will repeat together, 'Long Live The Emperor!'" They now had to meet the powerful challenge of an opposition which promised all the utopian joys the age could

imagine. They could no longer defeat them by the old system; so they had to outdo them at their own game and promise even more, with liberty to crown it. In this way did they become supporters of a Liberal Empire, which was thus created not by the opponents of Napoleon but by his old supporters, converted like him. They had the good fortune to find in Emile Ollivier a leader who had one of the rarest and most elevated minds of his day, and who was able to organize them and to bring their vague ambitions to success.

The Liberal Empire was an attempt to break the vicious circle of revolution and reaction in which France had been caught since Louis XVI. It sought to effect progress without revolution, in the belief that reforms could be obtained only gradually, whereas revolutions, being essentially violent, would never achieve their ends because they inevitably created new problems and brought divisions, emigrations and reaction in their train. It held that France could not turn at once from despotism to parliamentary government; and it established a representative form of government as a first step. It was not muddled thinking that led it to maintain that if France wished to imitate nineteenth-century England, she should first start by copying her neighbour's preliminary institutions of the seventeenth and eighteenth centuries.

It is possible to argue therefore that since Napoleon III tackled, and for a time successfully solved, the most fundamental problem in French politics, he can claim a place among the great statesmen of the century. When the prejudice against him has died down, it will very likely be recognized that he came near to achieving as much in politics as his uncle achieved in administration and in war.

RENÉ ARNAUD (1893–) represents a later and more responsible statement of republican views current much earlier in the Third Republic. The picture of Napoleon III that he provides is particularly unflattering. The emperor is portrayed as an unrealistic leader, a strange mixture of socialism and militarism. Arnaud views the Second Empire as morally deficient and the emperor as a dreamer, totally out of touch with reality. While many authors would accept the idea that Napoleon III was something of a dreamer, many would question whether these preoccupations were altogether impractical. Compare this selection in particular with that by Zeldin.*

The Second Republic and Napoleon III

This dreamer was typical of his day. Like everybody else, he had his system for reforming society and securing the welfare of the people. He believed in the extinction of pauperism through the triumph of democratic ideas. Uncultivated land was to be given to a huge association of workers, and the necessary credit allowed; between employers and employed an intermediary class of legally recognised "experts" was to be created, elected by the workers in the proportion of one to every ten of the latter; they were to be paid a double wage and would constitute the non-commissioned officers of the industrial army. What simple-minded faith in human action!

Theories with no foundation in reality, a burning desire for social reforms to complete the political reforms and secure true equality! It was all extremely "forty-eightish." But to it must be added that strange combination of militarism and socialism, of *"caporalism"* and humanitarian dreams, which might be expected in a Napoleon. . . . On the 20th of December he took an oath to remain true to the democratic Republic, one and indivisible; and of his own accord he added: "I shall regard as enemies of my country any who shall attempt by illegal means to change what France herself has established.". . . On the 20th of December, 1848, Prince Napoleon was un-

* Translated by E. F. Buckley and reprinted with permission from the 1937 edition of *The Second Republic and Napoleon III* by René Arnaud, G.P. Putnam's Sons, copyright, 1930.

doubtedly sincere. But human nature can be sincere in different and contradictory ways at different times.... During the first years of his Presidency he had bided his time, knowing that his hour would come. "I am convinced," he wrote to a lady friend in 1847, "that from time to time men are created, whom I shall call men of destiny, to whose hands the fate of their country is entrusted. And I believe that I myself am such a man.... If I am right, Providence will put me in a position to carry out my mission." Like his uncle, "The Other," he had faith in his star, a simple and superstitious faith. And strange to say, in a few years' time Destiny munificently granted his request and placed a crown upon the head of the poor exile riddled with debt. During these first years of his reign he was justified in thinking that the future lay in the hollow of his hand....

Unfortunately he was endowed with more heart than head, and was anything but clear-sighted. He had some sort of vague idea of the goal he was aiming at, but did not possess the lucidity calmly to consider ways and means of reaching it, nor was he able to foresee the consequences of his decisions. His was not the enlightened strength of will of the statesman, but the obstinacy of the weak man.... And he was too much of a fatalist really to be animated by a strong desire, being too sincere a believer, if not in the guidance of a divine providence, at least in the force of circumstances, to be able to blend them to his own will. The influence his immediate circle was able to exercise over such a man may well be imagined....

While the public mind was occupied in the contemplation of this pomp and splendour, the Emperor "governed through his Ministers." The latter used to meet twice a week, but the order of the day was decided by the Emperor himself, who put on the agenda only those subjects he thought it worth while to discuss. This ministerial council, which did not vote any measures or sign any documents, was an advisory committee and nothing more. The Emperor would listen, and after the meeting would come to a decision alone in his cabinet with the Minister concerned. He insisted on knowing everything and held himself alone responsible, the Minister having no power to act without his authority. But he soon saw that the mere desire to imitate Napoleon I was not sufficient to ensure success....

Thus by giving away to his sympathy with the idea of Italian unity and realising his grandiose dreams of new nationalities, the Emperor stirred up against him many people who had hitherto been his staunchest supporters. And in that same year, 1860, he also succeeded in rousing further hostility in a very different sphere through his passionate advocacy of Free Trade and his Anglomania. In the economic world, as in the world of religion, his airy schemes were opposed to certain established interests and provoked lively opposition. This political clumsiness, this incapacity to foresee results, this simple-minded hope of being able to hold within bounds an issue that he had himself let loose, and to guide a movement which he himself had created, this over-confident optimism of a blind and generous theorist, this love of utopias and chimeras—all this was both heart-rending and seductive, and explains why the *régime* was at once treated with great tolerance and exposed to the severest strictures. There was something of the "enlightened despot" about this "forty-eightish" Emperor. The pity of it is that those crowned dreamers who sincerely desire the welfare of their people, more often than not bring down all manner of disasters on their subjects even if they themselves escape. In any case, Napoleon III light-heartedly provoked the choler of numberless industrialists who had hitherto linked their prosperity with the fate of the Empire. Here again his airy theories were to cost him many a steadfast supporter.

France was protectionist by tradition. Colbert, Napoleon and Louis Philippe—a strange trio to be mentioned in one breath—had been inspired by the same doctrine in this respect; it was esssential for French industry to be protected against foreign competition by means of a whole system of prohibitive tariffs or high duties. . . .

But the Emperor had not abandoned his ideas. His friend, Michel Chevalier, an old St. Simonian, and Professor of Political Economy at the Collège de France, was giving lectures there in favour of Free Trade. He also contributed articles in the same strain to the *Débats.* . . . In the summer of 1859, Chevalier met Richard Cobden, the head of the Manchester School and the apostle of Free Trade, at a Congress held at Bradford. He also interviewed Mr. Gladstone, at that time Chancellor of the Exchequer, as a result of which Cobden visited Paris on a semi-official mission, though to prevent a scare the utmost secrecy was preserved. He was received at St. Cloud and dazzled the Emperor by depicting the advantages of Free Trade in glowing colours—the nations would mingle in friendly intercourse and there would be universal peace. Above all Cobden reminded the Emperor of Sir Robert Peel, the man who had

been responsible for reducing the duty on corn; and the inscription on his statue declaring that he had alleviated the lot of the working and suffering masses by lowering the price of prime necessities. This touched the heart of Napoleon III more than anything. For he sincerely desired the welfare of his people and was anxious to do all he could towards the *extinction of pauperism,* a subject which he had studied long ago in his prison at Ham. Thus the Emperor was won over. . . .

Resistance on the part of the Legislative Body was only to be expected. But by virtue of a *senatus consultum* of 1852, the Emperor had the right to sign treaties of commerce himself and introduce the changes in customs tariffs arranged for in such treaties without referring to the Legislative Body. Thus it was sufficient to draw up *in camera* a treaty with England to be able to apply the principles of Free Trade without let or hindrance with France's most important customer and source of supply. And negotiations were opened between Cobden and the English Ambassador in Paris on the one hand and Baroche, who was *ad interim* in charge of Foreign Affairs, and Rouher, the Minister of Commerce, on the other. The latter kept the matter dark from the officials in his own department, as well as from Magne, the Minister of Finance, who was known to be a protectionist and who would have had something to say on any matter affecting the customs. The affair had all the appearances of a conspiracy. It was only early in January 1860 that the English Press got wind of it. Whereupon the *Constitutionnel,* which had hitherto been protectionist, sang the praises of Free Trade, and, on the 15th of January, the *Moniteur* published a programme letter addressed by the Emperor to Fould, the Minister of State: "There is only one universal system of sound political economy which, by laying the foundations of national wealth, can spread comfort among the working classes...." This universal system was based upon the abolition of prohibitive tariffs, the establishment of moderate duties, and the conclusion of commercial treaties. But, by way of compensation, industry would be provided with better weapons for fighting foreign competition: "In order to encourage manufactures, all the raw materials—wool, cotton, etc.—indispensable to industry must be free of duty." Furthermore, the construction of canals, roads, and railways would be speeded up and an attempt made "to reduce tariffs by encouraging legitimate rivalry between the canals and the railways," and industry would be lent "the capital for perfecting its plant"—in short, an entire programme was drawn up for boldly encouraging French industry so that French manufactured goods, stuffs and cloths would be able to compete on equal terms with foreign industries.

This letter, which was meant to be reassuring, made a great stir in the industrial world. Four hundred manufacturers came to Paris from Flanders, Picardy, Normandy and Alsace and in vain solicited an audience of the Emperor. All they could do was to drawn up a vehement address which the Press had the courage to publish: "We are going to be condemned without having been granted a hearing...." Nevertheless, the Anglo-French treaty was signed on the 23rd of January, 1860.... And France was the Emperor. "I am the only man who knows what the foreign policy of France is going to be," he informed von der Goltz, recommending him to ignore newspaper opinions even when they were formulated by a Minister. The last illusion of greatness!...

Thus in a few hours, without a drop of blood being spilt, the *régime* for which seven million Frenchmen had voted *Yea* not four months previously fell to bits. It is true that only a third of Paris had voted for Napoleon III, and that once again it was Paris that had made the revolution. But who could possibly have defended the Empire which had just suffered such a terrible military disaster? The nation had not become Bonapartist, it had merely been following the Emperor "through inertia."... A band of adventurers had seized the power by means of a surprise attack on a certain December night in 1851, and had kept it by securing material prosperity and a semblance of glory for the country. And when the crisis arrived, instead of gathering in serried ranks about respected and beloved leaders, the people deserted a Government they had accepted only out of weakness, while the imperial edifice, deprived of its natural bulwark, the army, crumbled to bits almost of its own accord, like a castle of cards under the flick of a child's fingers.

The Reverend FREDERICK ARTHUR SIMPSON (1883–), Fellow and Dean of Trinity College, Cambridge, has written two thorough books on Louis Napoleon, constituting the first major objective study of the emperor. Simpson's conclusions regarding Napoleon III have been generally sympathetic, and his suggestion that the Second Empire was more important than the First has helped to establish the period as worthy of more research. In this excerpt, we can see how Louis Napoleon gave conspiratorial overtones to a perfectly honest incident, and we may ponder to what extent such tactics have mislead historians.*

Louis Napoleon and the Recovery of France, 1848–1856

For personal issues apart, from the standpoint of European and universal history the First Empire, as compared with the Second, was an episode. Both its victories and its defeats were, by the side of its successor's, sterile; and colossal as were its commotions they were as a whole singularly barren of proportionate and permanent result. For in general they evoked reactions strong enough, but only strong enough, to overwhelm them. Hence the whole affair ended at Vienna in an order which was as nearly a successful "As you were" as any which has ever been issued in History.

Wholly different were the consequences of the Second Empire. Its triumphs too were transitory: but its transit left both the map and the moral order of Europe revolutionised. The Europe of 1815 and the Europe of 1789 were neither in ponderables nor imponderables so far apart as the Europe which contained and the Europe which lacked the new Italy, the new Germany, and the temporal power of the Pope. . . . Directly or indirectly Napoleon has been credited with giving an impetus to any nationalist movement which later in the nineteenth century succeeded, just as he would have been pronounced to have rendered inevitable the success of Poland, had she not failed. . . . Anybody can attribute a deed to the doer of it: it takes an historian to trace it back to its opponents of some previous generation. Yet

* Reproduced by permission of Longmans, Green & Co. Ltd. from *Louis Napoleon and the Recovery of France, 1848–1856* (London, 1923), by F.A. Simpson.

even for historians the time is approaching when it will be permissible to recognise, that the most fruitful act after all of the First Empire was the begetting of posthumous issue in the Second. For the Second Empire itself is nearly remote enough now to seem a respectable spiritual ancestor.... It is moreover increasingly clear that without the unexpected aid of one sincere friend at court the struggling and unorthodox cause of nationality could not have achieved its unexpected triumphs: and to have presented such a cause with such an ally is the historic function of the Second Empire.

But even on purely personal grounds its mournful and enigmatic ruler presents a challenging figure to posterity.... No ruler of France—none perhaps of any European country—was so cosmopolitan in his training and outlook as Napoleon III. None certainly was less French. Essentially he was an international figure: too good a citizen perhaps of Europe to be the ultimately successful ruler of any one country in it. The dreams and broodings of South Germany, the sleepy dignity of the Dutch, the slow speech and kindliness of England, the secretiveness and fatalism of the Italy he so loved —these were his, and a compassion for the people and a humanitarian idealism that were not peculiarly French.... It was a matter not immaterial or barren of result, that for fifteen momentous years the hegemony of Europe should be transferred from Russia to France, from Nicholas to Napoleon III. Alike during the Great Reaction which followed the downfall of the First Empire, and the Armed Peace which succeeded upon the overthrow of the Second, the control of European politics was in the hands of men to whom the fact that a given condition of affairs existed was strong if not all-sufficient reason that it should con-

tinue so to exist. Whether by an inviolable international agreement in the past, or by a precarious balance of power in the present; whether based upon theoretical principle before Louis Napoleon's rise or maintained by practical expedience after his fall, the whole official diplomacy of Europe tended in either period to the maintenance of existing frontiers because they existed. But between these two periods there intervened another strangely different; wherein Europe was dominated by a man in whose case all ordinary rules of diplomacy were not merely suspended but reversed. The ordinary monarch, born on the footsteps of the throne, comes somewhat easily by the conclusion that what is, is right: half a lifetime's exile and proscription had engendered in the mind of this particular ruler a fixed idea that what was, was wrong. And for other and more concrete reasons the *status quo,* to the conventional diplomatist little less than a fetish, was to Louis Napoleon a thing positively repellent. To Louis Napoleon, as to his opponents, the *status quo* spelt the Congress of Vienna; but to him that Congress stood for the downfall of his dynasty and the humiliation of his country. Hence to him there was always an initial presumption not against but in favour of change....

But to these natural incentives inclining Louis Napoleon to supersede the Congress of Vienna other and more disinterested motives were added. Whatever service the Congress of Vienna had rendered to Europe in the past by the establishment of a lasting order and peace, that order was now visibly outworn. Many of its provisions had from the first been imposed upon unwilling peoples; and the increasing hardship inflicted on them by the rigid maintenance of an obsolete system had produced in the complex and brooding mind of Louis

Napoleon a genuine sympathy . . . For
thirty years he had gazed at the sullen
surface of European politics, pent and
damned by Metternich and his system
into one stagnant and unruffled pond.
And as he gazed he had become possessed
with the desire at all costs to stir up its
leaden depths. . . . Interested and disinterested motives here propelled him in the
same direction. With an adventurer's
natural detestation of routine, a wan-
derer's inherent appetite for change,
Louis Napoleon stood by instinct, interest, and conviction for the precise anti-
thesis of all the cherished changelessness
of the preceding age.

Hence for the failures of 1848 no compensation was to prove so valuable as
the success of Louis Napoleon. . . . By
making himself supreme in France, and
France once more ascendant in Europe,
he was to secure for Europe a period in
which the shackles of diplomatic order
and routine were so far loosened as to
allow of much that in the generation
before or after had been impossible. So
long and so long only as a crowned
adventurer held sway in Paris, were adventures to be permitted in the sphere
of international politics all Europe over.
During the reign of this imperial
dreamer, and during it alone, did the
conditions of nineteenth-century diplomacy allow dreamers to translate their
dreams into action. This fact, naturally
hidden from contemporary observation,
suffices to give permanent importance to
the conflicts by means of which Louis
Napoleon won first a fleeting supremacy
for himself in France, and then a supremacy as fleeting for France in Europe.
. . . They served no less a purpose than
to render possible a period in which all
things were possible: a period into which
enterprises of great pith and moment
must pack themselves, or lose the name
of action; a period into which was in

fact compressed almost whatever of vital
change the century had witnessed since
Waterloo. . . .

In point of fact Louis did attempt to
induce Lamartine himself, the very personification of French idealist republicanism, to become his first premier. The
scene and manner of their interview were
entirely typical of the prince's methods.
He had spent the first day after his election in unsuccessful attempts to form a
ministry of all the talents and had met
with a series of rebuffs. At the close of
a long day of formal and fruitless nego-
tiation, he lost patience and resolved
upon a direct personal appeal to Lamartine. "Without warning me," wrote Lamartine in his memoirs, "the Prince
flung himself upon his horse at nightfall
and galloped towards my house in the
Bois de Boulogne," accompanied only
by one friend. Halting himself "in a
dark pine alley in the neighborhood,"
he sent forward the single friend who
accompanied him to urge Lamartine to
meet him there at once for a secret interview." "I had just sat down to dinner.
. . . I immediately ordered by horse to be
saddled and rode off with him to meet
the Prince as if by chance. It was night,
and there was no longer another horse-
man but ourselves in the wood. . . ."

And so in the heart of that desolate
place—for it was Louis Napoleon himself
who was later to convert this wilderness
into a garden—the President and Lamartine were left to their interview; for all
the world like a couple of highwaymen
plotting nocturnal assault upon some
opulent wayfarer. Their actual business
was honest and respectable enough; but
it pleased Louis even when he was not
conspiring to have the *mise en scène* of
a conspiracy: night, and a secret assigna-
tion under the most sombre tree that
grows; black pines towering into a stark
December sky. It formed indeed an

entirely characteristic conclusion to his first day's work as Ruler of France, this sudden refreshing plunge from the routine of office, which though new was already tedious, into the old childish delight of mysterious adventure; none the less characteristic that the deed done in the dark might just as well have been done by day; none the less characteristic that the nocturnal interview ended without solid results. . . .

The practical achievements of the opening months of Louis Napoleon's official life were obvious alike to his countrymen and to foreign observers of his career. It was far otherwise with two notable attempts made by the new President during these same months to give effect to the grandiose dreams of his long political exile. Both attempts failed, through lack of English co-operation. . . .

It is a matter of common knowledge that in the last year of his reign Louis Napoleon's government endeavoured to concert some scheme for the limitation of armaments with Prussia, the only military rival of France. But it has hitherto escaped the notice of historians that in the first month of his official life Louis himself was the author of the most drastic proposal for the limitation of naval armaments ever put forward by the head of any nation. At this time, and for forty years to come, France was the only country in existence whose fleet in any way approximated to that of Great Britain: the naval armaments of the other powers were inconsiderable. On January 17, Louis Napoleon caused his newly appointed Minister for Foreign Affairs, Drouyn de Lhuys, to propose to Normanby, the British ambassador, that the two Western Powers should take common action in regard to the limitation of their navies. The French Government would, said Drouyn, "be prepared to make almost any reduction we might

suggest, provided we were disposed to do so upon somewhat the same relative scale"; adding "that so long as England and France thoroughly understood each other their reduced fleets would be quite sufficient to ensure the respect of the rest of the world." Louis Napoleon himself formally repeated the offer to Normanby in a subsequent interview with him.

Palmerston was apparently somewhat at a loss as to how to deal with such an unprecedented proposal: he expressed himself as gratified by the proof of friendly feeling shown by the President in his overture; but stated that it was impossible for England with its world-wide possessions to make its fleet dependent on the size of the fleet maintained by any one Power. Thus the door was politely closed upon a proposal which might have produced beneficent results for both nations, had it received a somewhat different treatment. For the rivalry in ship-building which it was designed to avert did in fact take place between the two nations in the later years of the Second Empire. Yet on Louis' part the proposal was no mere passing whim: six years later, in the course of the Crimean War, his conversations with Cowley show the persistence of the same idea. On the present occasion, in spite of England's refusal to co-operate, the President resolved that France should make on her own account a beginning at any rate in the process of disarmament: in the teeth of considerable opposition he succeeded in effecting large reductions both in men and material in the naval and military budget of 1849.

Some six weeks later Palmerston quashed remorselessly a second of Louis Napoleon's visionary suggestions. On the 5th of March 1849, the President proposed to the British ambassador that the two governments should issue a united invitation to the powers for a general congress to deal with all questions which threatened to disturb the peace of Europe. Louis proposed the scheme in a confidential interview, and without any previous consultation of his cabinet. At present, he said, the only hope of maintaining order was based on appeals to treaties of 1815: but these treaties had been violated over and over again by almost every one of the contracting powers: attempts to patch up peace in every part of Europe upon such an outworn basis could hardly be expected to prove successful. Among other advantages of the scheme Louis Napoleon urged, that in any such new congress for the modification of the treaties of 1815, France would be able to co-operate on equal terms with the other Powers: naturally she had always regarded the original Congress of Vienna with some aversion, but after sharing on equal terms in such a congress as Louis now proposed she would be able to give her whole-hearted support to the cause of order based on treaties she had herself assisted in revising. The suggestion of "modification" of these several treaties evidently served however to arouse Palmerston's suspicions, and he had little difficulty, with every appearance of goodwill, in crushing the project....

Although his new legislature was elected at the end of February and at work by the end of March, Louis could not restrain his desire for action even for those few weeks.... For two months he revelled in the activities of a beneficent despot.... His activities in this respect during the opening months of 1852 were such as to appease the most insatiate appetite for infallible direction from above; during those months the French *père de famille* could never open his morning's newspaper without lighting on some new decree of indefatigable author-

ity. One day's decree converted the national debt from a 5 per cent. to a 4½ per cent. loan.... Other decrees established a great network of railways throughout France. The Orleanist regime had generally discouraged and invariably delayed enterprise of this kind: Louis now gave it a sudden and on the whole a well-directed impulse, with the result that the total length of French railways was quadrupled in the next seven years. Private enterprise alone was employed, with no State subvention or guarantee: but the President stipulated that at the close of ninety-nine years all such property should revert to the State. Succeeding decrees multipled in a similar manner roads, canals, telegraph lines, and harbours. Others followed to check the adulteration of food, discountenance Sunday labour, and to improve the sanitation of slums.

In every case the word was no sooner spoken that the work was begun; like Aladdin newly endowed with his wishing ring, Louis not only took childish delight in multiplying the activities of his genius, but he would have his behests executed with all imaginable celerity....

Unfortunately Louis Napoleon, as fairy prince in the pantomime of these winter months, was not content to seek his effects solely amid the oriental splendours of the Arabian Nights; from the rôle of Aladdin he could not resist a temporary excursion to the part of Robin Hood.

It was the immense possessions of the Orleanist princes which now tempted him to the part—at all times somewhat congenial to him—of benevolent highwayman. In compelling the exiled king to sell within twelve months all real property he possessed in France, Louis was only following the precedent set by Bourbons in their treatment of the Bonapartes, and by Orleanists in their treatment of the Bourbons. But no similar justification could be pleaded for another decree published on the same day. It was an ancient and established principle that upon his accession all the private property of any French prince, by whatever title acquired, became merged instantly in the Crown domain. But Louis Philippe by a legal fiction had evaded this rule; making over to his sons, on the very day of his election to the throne, the greater portion of his enormous landed estates; excluding from the gift his eldest son, and reserving to himself a life interest in all property thus transferred. The expedient itself had been of doubtful legality: by a step at least equally dubious in law and far more high-handed in its incidence, Louis now denounced the previous transference; and declared the estates in question restored to the State domain, from which he pronounced them to have been illegally alienated. A few Legitimists, in their detestation of Louis Philippe, rejoiced at the proceeding; but the Orleanists, as was natural, bitterly resented it. . . .

. . . The President proceeded gaily to apply his booty to a score of benevolent purposes; among them the endowment of mutual benefit societies, the provision of decent Christian burial free of charge for the poor, the establishment of orphanages and asylums, the improvement of workmen's dwellings in large manufacturing towns, and the foundation in the *crédit foncier* societies of a really useful system of agricultural loan and mortgage banks, by means of which the impoverished landowner was enabled to make long-needed improvements in his small estate. Upon these followed decrees for the provision of public baths and wash-houses, the improvement of hospitals, the reorganisa-

tion of pawn-shops in the interests of their *clientèle,* and the reform of the *Bureaux de placements* in such a sense as to make of them a sort of primitive labour exchange. Doubtless Louis imagined that by his act he was creating a multitude of vested interests in France hostile to the Orleanist dynasty, or at any rate financially interested in its continued exclusion from the throne. But naturally the proceeding was regarded as a strange inconsistency in one who had just appealed to France as the defender of private property against the onslaughts of socialism. . . .

. . . Festivities and banquets, decorations and promotions gave to the passing days an air of universal triumph. In dispensing these hospitalities and honours the Emperor took evident delight. To ask a couple of generals to dinner, and at dessert rise and toast them suddenly as Marshals, to be the centre and source of the general festivities, this was at once the sign and satisfaction of his own success. Sometimes however he made these banquets the occasion of more serious pronouncements. At this juncture the project of a Suez Canal was beginning to take substance in the teeth of the bitter hostility of Palmerston, De Redcliffe and Lord John Russell, who fought the scheme stubbornly at every stage, denouncing the canal until it was half-dug as impracticable, and then with even greater vehemence as opposed to the highest interests of Turkey and of Egypt. With these the interests of England chanced to coincide: since the canal obscurely, but all the more dangerously for that, constituted a menace to her Indian Empire. To the overcoming of obstacles raised by this opposition Lesseps was now devoting the same unconquerable optimism which throughout his life was both his strength and snare. In the present instance, more fortunate than in his earlier or later undertakings, he could count on the whole-hearted support of Louis Napoleon. To this the Emperor testified... "that he took the greatest possible interest in the scheme, which seemed to him a universal benefit; that he had studied it in all its aspects and acquainted himself with all the documents bearing on it, and earnestly wished its success. But the enterprise, admirable as it was in every way, had given rise to certain objections and obstructions, especially in England. For his part he could not consider that these objections were well-founded, and he quite hoped to see them removed. At the same time he was not disposed to rush matters, for fear of compromising their success. Instead, relying upon the happy alliance which united the two peoples, he looked to the future—and to a very near future—for an agreement upon this question." In such an utterance Napoleon III was seen at his best: sustaining, as he did not always sustain, a remote and beneficient design with a statesmanlike appreciation of the proper method for its attainment. To this policy he adhered with admirable persistence and good temper; as when three years later after some particularly discouraging despatch from London he gave Lesseps an interview, told him not to worry, "you can count on my support and protection," but added, "It is a squall: we must shorten sail." It would have been well for Louis Napoleon if he could always have pursued his own dreams with the same combination of undiscouraged idealism and practical common sense. As it was the opening of the Suez Canal by the Empress was destined to furnish his chequered reign with almost the last and certainly not the least-deserved of its triumphs.

For the moment deserved and undeserved good fortunes seemed to pile themselves upon him. As the fall of Sevastopol had crowned the first great exhibition of Paris, so the Congress of Paris was to receive what to the French Emperor himself must have been yet a more signal benediction. On March 16 a child was born to him, and that child a son. Twice before he had been disappointed of that hope; now it seemed that the Prince had postponed his coming only that he might receive a yet more imperial welcome. Three years earlier, socially boycotted in his own capital, and in the eyes of foreign courts a very dubious adventurer indeed, Louis Napoleon had contracted a marriage which to the delight of all his enemies seemed to have set the final seal upon his ostracism. His boldest friend would not then have dared to predict, that the son born of that marriage would find awaiting him an inheritance scarcely inferior in its seeming splendour and security to that which Napoleon himself had won for the first Prince Imperial of France. In extent the new Empire was in no way comparable to the old, but under it France had become once more the first nation of the world. Unaugmented in territory it had received in the last two years an immense increase in prestige; victories infinitely less brilliant than those of the First Empire had yet sufficed to obtain for it a European sanction and a semblance of stability such as that Empire had never been able to possess. Indeed the one thing that now seemed lacking to it was an heir.

It was at six o'clock on the morning of March 16 that the cannon of the Invalides once more echoed through Paris: not the mere one and twenty that should suffice for a girl; but a full salute of a hundred and one guns, proclaiming that the Emperor had indeed a son. The dramatic effect of this distinction was wasted, since Paris still slept: but when it did awake to the news its rejoicings were instant, spontaneous, and all but universal. This "universality of the manifestation" was the feature that most impressed the *Times* correspondent as he walked round the illuminated city in the evening, even in "back streets and lanes where I believe no lights were ever hung before." No more striking contrast could have been conceived than that between the forced and official celebrations which had greeted the bride, and the genuine enthusiasm evoked by arrival of the heir. That arrival had been none of the easiest. For eighteen hours on end the state bodies had been in permanent session: while the Emperor during the prolonged sufferings of the Empress had been pacing the palace in an agony of apprehension. Nor were his fears ungrounded; both mother and child were in imminent danger of death.

It chanced that the Prince's birthday was Palm Sunday: and for text that morning the court chaplain took the familiar sentence, *"Beatus qui venit in nomine Domini"*: applying it, in words careless of precedent or consequence, to the triumphal entry of this new prince into his capital. Perhaps as he listened the Emperor may have thought of exits as well as entrances; certainly his own far more subdued response to the congratulations of his senators two days later seemed to display a desire to "touch wood." In the baptismal register after his son's names he had written the words *Fils de France*. On this title he now dilated. "It was," he said, "a revival from the usage of the *ancien régime;* but not for that reason a meaningless piece of antiquarianism. For truly, gentlemen, when an heir is born to perpetuate a national institution, that child is something more than the scion of a family; he is the whole country's son; and this name of his points him to his duties." Then after urging that for a

Napoleon, the elect of the people, this title must mean not less but more than for the children of the ancient kings, he put into words a thought which even if unspoken could hardly have been absent from the minds of his hearers. For more than two centuries the crown of France had not passed once in direct succession from father to son. And now who was Louis Napoleon, and what was this his child, that he should hope to escape their common fate? Another memory, more recent and particular, pressed still more insistently on all. Not fifty years ago another Child of France had been cradled in Paris: born amid every circumstance of imperial splendour; yet destined to die childless and his father's only child, an exile and an exile's son, the last direct descendant of a deposed and discredited dynasty.

No present splendour could quite have banished from men's mind such memories as those. But in such case the common course would have been silence from ill-omened words. The utterances of the present Emperor however were rarely commonplace. In the days of his own long exile and imprisonment, despite the utter prostration of his fortunes, he had proclaimed insistently his unalterable conviction that he would live to rule France. But now that his highest dreams seemed realised; assured not of Empire only, but of peace, of victory, of a son; himself all powerful in a country which his own rule had made once more the first Power in Europe; now he spoke only with a tentative and melancholy modesty, as though he who from the depths had foreseen the height, from the height also foresaw the *débâcle*. Not all the acclamations, he said, which surrounded the cradle of his son, could prevent him from pondering on the destiny of those born in the same place under like circumstances. "If," continued the Emperor, "I hope that his will be a happier fate, it is because trusting in God I cannot doubt that protection, when I see Him raise up again, by a marvellous combination of circumstances, all that it had pleased Him to beat down forty years ago: as though He wished to strengthen, by martyrdom and misfortune, the new dynasty which had issued from the ranks of the people. History too," he continued, with a plain reference to the fate alike of the First Empire and of the Orleanist regime, "history has lessons that I shall not forget. It teaches me that the favours of fortune must never be abused; it teaches me too that a dynasty can only hope for stability by remaining faithful to its origin, and by devoting itself entirely to the popular interests, for whose service it was created." The speech ended with a hope of better things. "This child whose birth was consecrated by the peace, by the blessing of the Pope telegraphed within an hour of his birth, by the acclamations of the French people whom the Emperor loved so well—this child will I hope prove worthy of the destinies that await him." The reply "created considerable emotion" among its immediate hearers: in a similar strain later in the day the Emperor responded to the congratulations of the plenipotentiaries of the Peace Congress. "I am happy," he said, "that Providence has granted me a son at a moment when an era of general reconciliation is dawning upon Europe. I will bring him up imbued with the idea that nations must not be egotistical, and that the peace of Europe depends upon the prosperity of every nation."

A fortnight after the birth and baptism of the Prince, the delegates of the Congress of Paris met to attach their names to the issue of their labours: signing at midday on March 30 the formal treaty of peace. This too was on a Sunday: and for this occasion as for the last French Catholics discovered, in the twice repeated *Pax vobiscum* of the Gospel, a happy coincidence in the liturgy for the day. In this case the coincidence was more than accidental; since but for it the protestations of Clarendon and Cowley on behalf of their country against the signing of the peace on Sunday might not improbably have prevailed. As it was, fearing that further opposition might cause real umbrage, they finally consented to this small outrage upon Protestant opinion. That opinion had been in no way especially perturbed by the Sunday slaughter of Inkerman: perhaps after all it might be lawful to make peace also on the Sabbath.

Hence without further ado the treaty was signed and sealed. . . . "Turning to Lord Cowley and Lord Clarendon he added, that peace had been rendered possible by the spirit of conciliation they had exhibited." As a result "it was clearly understood by the Congress that in the opinion of the Emperor the question of peace and war had rested with England." For the rest the speech expressed satisfaction that the present peace was one which a great nation could accept without degradation: and therefore formed a settlement affording reasonable hope of real permanence and stability. In part this was perhaps an answering gesture to the many flattering overtures which the Russian diplomatists throughout the negotiations had not ceased to make towards the Emperor: in part it was certainly a hinted reference —the sole complacency which Napoleon III permitted himself—to the now discarded provisions of Vienna.

The note of triumph in the Emperor's speech was so modest as scarcely to be perceptible, but matter for it was obvious to all. Forty-two years ago on that very day, Paris had capitulated to the armies of the allies; at whose head on the morrow Alexander of Russia had ridden in triumph through the conquered capital. And now not only had this position been reversed, but the new Alexander had even deigned to make the memories of that contrast the basis of an appeal to the new Napoleon. "The Emperor Alexander"—so he had suffered his trusted emissary Seebach to remark—"the Emperor Alexander counts upon the Emperor Napoleon III taking the same interest in his fate, as his uncle the Emperor Alexander took in the fate of Napoleon I." Nor was this all. Less than four years ago the Czar Nicholas had haughtily refused to accord to this upstart Emperor the customary salutation of kings: now his son and successor was pressing upon Louis the highest royal order of his realm, and pressing it in vain; even though he offered to come to Paris himself in order to perform the investiture in person. It would have been difficult to imagine a reversal more signal and complete.

And this reversal Louis might well regard as something more than a personal or dynastic success; in some measure at any rate it stood for a truly national triumph. Seven years earlier France had taken him, outcast and exiled, and raised him up to be her ruler. But in those seven years he also might almost claim, that what the French people had done for him in France, he himself had done for France in Europe. France too, in his own words, had formerly been "disinherited of her rank in the councils of Europe:" now she was "prosperous, peaceful, and respected." So far as the external situation was concerned, this was no more than the truth: from being the outcast he had made her in effect the arbiter of Europe.

Internally the matter was more doubtful. The success achieved by Louis' speeches from the throne had other causes than their intrinsic excellence, or even than the height to which he had raised that rostrum in Europe. At least in part they owed their acclamation to the echoing silence which their author had himself secured for them; down which, as down deserted corridors, his oracular utterances rang mournfully and alone. The eminence of his own political position in France was the result in large part of the absence from public life of all eminence besides. That absence he himself recognised and deplored; only a few weeks ago he had lamented to Cowley "that there were no statesmen in France." Such an admission at the time was striking enough. For so high stood the prestige of the imperial diplomacy at the moment that the Comte de Chambord himself in a letter to a friend expressed the intention of availing himself in the event of his restoration of all the ability which surrounded the Emperor. The letter was intercepted and shown to Louis Napoleon. "All the ability which surrounds me!" was his comment: "he won't reign long if that is all he can count on." In neither case did the Emperor show any sign of recognising the cause, even in the act of realising the result. Eighteen months earlier a remark of his to the Duke of Newcastle had displayed a more just appreciation of the position. "Former governments," he said, "tried to reign by the support of perhaps one million of the educated classes. I have tried to lay hold of the other twenty-nine." The claim was justified, for the attempt was certainly made and made with considerable success. Broadly speaking, it is true that the more aristocratic governments which preceded and followed the Second Empire had neither its care nor its attraction for the common people. But fatally true also was the admission which Louis' very claim implied. He had brought the twenty and nine from the wilderness and lost the one million that mattered. For that one outraged and righteous million included almost all the political and diplomatic experience, above all, all the eloquence of France.

It was across this gap and emptiness immediately encircling his throne that Louis Napoleon had to fling his utterances to his people. . . . Single-handed he was forced to attempt work which was utterly beyond his strength. Even in 1856 his intimates were aware that the price was increasing physical ill-health. But here it was the essential vice of the imperial system that this price he could not pay alone. . . . It was indeed the tragedy of the reign, that the Emperor's illness allowed him just time enough to acquire the strongest hand in Europe; and then intervened to disable him from playing it even tolerably. "It was a very sad sight," wrote Prince Albert's brother, describing a visit which he paid to Emperor just after the fall of Sevastopol, "to see this man, who knew himself just arrived at the summit of his position, and secured in the possession of his power, in a state of the plainest physical decay." Never in fact had any ruler of France more brilliant chances than those which Louis Napoleon had won for his country at the end of the first half of his reign. And never were advantages more miserably thrown away.

The turning-point however was not yet. Although his disease was already harder upon him than men knew, the Emperor had left another five years in which he was only exceptionally under its sway, before the longer period when it was exceptional for him to be free from it. And in the interval he was to put his hand to a task which no other hand

than his would have attempted, and no lesser help than his could have achieved. That task was the Liberation of Italy.

The history of that work—by far the most considerable achievement of Louis Napoleon's life—we hope to recount elsewhere. Meanwhile we may take our leave of him at the apparent pinnacle of his fortunes: successful abroad, and for the moment, save in the Orleanist salons, popular even in Paris; while from the provinces he could command a veritable devotion. There was no power on the Continent that would not welcome his alliance: for the moment he seems almost to have justified Cousin's description of him as the "Emperor of Europe." Hitherto "the Emperor" *sans phrase* meant Nicholas: henceforth it meant Napoleon. The implied hegemony had not been easily won; but once attained its retention would seem to have been a relatively easy matter, especially for a ruler both schooled in person by adversity and profoundly convinced by his uncle's fate of the need of moderation in good fortune. Common prudence, and the abstinence from further fantastic adventure, seemed all that was now needed to secure for his reign a montonously prosperous conclusion, with all the posthumous titles of statesmanship which history awards easily to final political success.

That choice was not made, nor those prizes gained. But the career is perhaps not less worth following for that. The habit of seeking change pursued Louis Napoleon even when change was become to his own disadvantage; but it was other men's ills as well as his own good that he could not leave alone. And for this reason the expenditure and exhaustion of his power was a process in many ways more fruitful than the acquisition of it, although it led him eventually to astonish by his failures a world which had hardly ceased to be amazed by his success.

The author of works in intellectual history and two
volumes on the 1815–1830 period, FREDERICK B.
ARTZ (1894–   ) of Oberlin College discusses below,
in an article written at the outset of World War II,
some unsavory features of Napoleonic dictatorship.
Artz is particularly unimpressed by Napoleon III's
career; compare his views with the later selection by
Pouthas. Is Artz really writing about Napoleon III or
about Hitler? Although the author has also anticipated
some of the ideas propounded by Namier, his general
approach—valuing Napoleon III's empire as a shabby
counterfeit product—carries a familiar republican ring.*

Bonapartism and Dictatorship

A series of pamphlets which Louis
Napoleon began to publish after 1832
elaborated the gospel of St. Helena and
mixed with it currents of the republicanism and the socialism of the time....
In the most important of these, the
"Napoleonic Ideas" of 1839, Napoleon I
appears as the apostle of democracy who
had lacked only time to complete his program of removing restrictions on freedom and establishing a parliamentary
regime. If the Empire were ever re-
established, it would carry on and complete this liberalizing work. The Restoration had been the government of the
nobles, the July Monarchy was the regime of the middle class, a new Bonapartist Empire would be for the good
of all. Let the people rule! Like Napoleon I, his nephew maintained that an
emperor elected by plebiscite expressed
the national will better than could any
parliament. A pamphlet on the extinction of pauperism which showed Saint-
Simonian influence, proposed the re-
clamation of waste land by state-aided
agricultural colonies. In all this, socialism was mixed with nationalism, militarism, democracy, and dictatorship.
"The name Napoleon," he declared in
1849, "is a complete program in itself;
it stands for order, authority, religion,
the welfare of the people within; without
for national dignity."

* From Frederick B. Artz, "Bonapartism and Dictatorship," *South Atlantic Quarterly,*
XXXIX, no. 1 (January 1940). Copyright by the Duke University Press. Used by permission.

Publicity and martyrdom were doing a strange work. They first spread a fantastic myth which presented Napoleon I as the friend of peace, the supporter of religion, and the champion of nationality and of democracy, and second, they turned attention to his nephew, a young adventurer who was the living embodiment of the myth.... To some of the Catholics he seemed a champion of the Papacy, to many of the Socialists he appealed as a friend of the poor, to the capitalists he appeared the bulwark against socialism and to some of the republicans—who should have known better—he seemed the champion of popular sovereignty and of the revolutionary ideals.... [S]o extensive was his backing that it was a stupid mistake to carry through his "coup" with quite unnecessary repression. He then appealed to the "one sovereign I recognize in France —the people" as had his uncle, and a plebiscite, overwhelmingly favorable, accepted his coup d'état....

Napoleon III gave the working class some improved housing, co-operative banks and stores, some old age and accident insurance, and finally the right to form trade unions and to strike. He had roads and canals improved, large areas drained and brought under cultivation; the railroads increased sixfold, and the steam force utilized by industry more than quintupled. Hausman rebuilt Paris. Most of the provincial cities were extensively overhauled. Napoleon III, like his uncle, tried to regulate the economic life of his state; the regulations of the Second Empire show some regard for the working man, though with both Napoleons the advantage was always on the side of capital.

These wholesale ameliorations characterized both the First and the Second Empires, though it should never be forgotten that Napoleon III created nothing comparable to the Codes, the Concordat, the Université de France, the Bank of France or the administrative system of the First Napoleon. Both emperors were, in some degree, trying to distract men from the loss of their liberties.... Both regimes, though they were despotic, made concessions to the spirit of the time and set up fake parliamentary institutions. These lath-and-plaster assemblies, one of which could debate bills without voting and another which might vote without debating, gave to the regimes the appearance of democratic virtues while the tyrant enjoyed the solid satisfactions of dictatorship. The real work of governing was in the hands of the Council of State—on which Mussolini's Grand Council is modeled—and the prefects. The Council of State was a body of men eminent in technical knowledge, who transacted a huge amount of business in secret.... Next to the Emperor this council was the central motive force of the whole machine, but the Emperor's constant attention was necessary. So completely did both the First and Second Empires depend upon the will of the dictator that had either emperor been seriously ill for a month the whole Empire would have sickened....

When Napoleon returned from Elba in 1815, he had granted France a liberal constitution, the "Acte Additionnel." This deathbed gesture of the first Napoleon had been made a cardinal feature in the apocalyptic campaign of Saint Helena and had formed a sort of Paradise Regained theme in the pamphleteering of Louis Napoleon. So after the Italian War of 1859, when the old appeals were failing, Napoleon III, the perfect adventurer, drew a new arrow from his quiver,

"L'Empire Libéral." Actually the liberalizing of the regime between 1860 and 1870 was undertaken in order to rally support for the failing forces of the Second Empire. One lot of dictatorial ballast after another was thrown out; in 1860 the deputies were granted the right of drawing up an answer to the emperor's annual address; a year later they were allowed to vote the budget by sections. In 1867 the deputies were permitted to question the ministers, and the censorship of the press was relaxed. Finally, in 1869 and 1870 the Legislative Body was allowed to initiate laws and the ministry was made responsible to parliamentary control. But four months after Napoleon III said, "the edifice has been crowned with liberty...," the Second Empire itself had collapsed at Sedan. It would probably not have lasted anyway; its mistakes and its humiliations were too numerous, its secret police had alienated the workers, the concessions to parliamentarianism were made too late, and the regime of Napoleon III had lived too long in sin ever to become respectable. Moreover, no real collaboration would have been possible between men who loathed liberty and men who detested the Empire....

Stendhal's comment that one of the chief reasons for the fall of the First Empire was Napoleon I's taste for mediocrities is still more apt of the Second Empire. In the case of the Second Empire, the inner circle fell to knifing each other; the administration became, as one writer says, "a crate of crabs." Both emperors on whom everything depended showed declining powers in the later years of their rule.... Napoleon III, for the last half of his rule, suffered terribly with gall stones and was physically a man slowly falling into ruin....

Beside the story of the fall of the First Empire that of the Second seems like a cheap and pirated edition. Louis Napoleon's domestic policy, as we have seen, had been a fair success, but in 1859 he set forth on a foreign policy well intentioned, but one in which he was outplayed by the statesmen of other powers and in which he raised up at home one set of enemies after another. All his plans were shot through with a strange political dilettantism which harbored a fantastic mixture of mirages and utopias.... Both Napoleons failed to enlist the intelligence or wisely to use the labors of one of the most gifted and energetic of modern peoples. They betrayed a great trust and brought down ruin on themselves and on their people.

ROBERT SENCOURT (1894–), a pseudonym for
Robert Esmond Gordon George, has written, among
his other works, an excellent biography of the Empress
Eugenie. His book on Napoleon III follows the
generally favorable interpretation already established
by Simpson. Though Sencourt's study is based on a
wider range of documents, it is perhaps marred by an
excessive enthusiasm for his subject. Portraying the
emperor as ahead of his age, a man of our times rather
than his own, Sencourt works out a theme you will
have found implied in the earlier reading by Aubry.
Again, in the selection by Roger Williams, the student
will find Napoleon III presented as out of touch with
his era—but, in contrast to Sencourt, Williams will
place him as a century late, as a man whose attitudes
belong more to the eighteenth century.*

Napoleon III: The Modern Emperor

Sedan! But surely there was more than
Sedan. Had the dying man looked back
on the twenty-two years of his dictatorship, what scenes he could evoke! He
who had wandered so far in Italy as an
insurgent, and who had languished so
long in prison and in exile could recall
experiences as brilliant as those of Mal-
maison and the Conquerer. He could
hear again the great shouts which greeted
his first progress in the South; he could
see the old veterans crowding back to
worship him, he could hear the chisp-
chasp of the trodden leaves as, with the
young Countess de Teba on horseback
beside him, he rode over them in the
Forest of Fontainebleau; he could see the
Queen of England bending at Windsor
to fix the Garter to his knee; the King
of Sardinia riding at his side through
the streets of Milan that his aid had
won; the christening of his heir in Notre-
Dame, with a Pope and a King as god-
fathers; the Lake of Annecy surrounded
by its mountains which he had made
French, . . . the thick lips of Princess Metternich, after she had made one of those
audacious sallies which for forty years
after his fall were still to be the wonder
of Vienna, and which for ten years were
the highest salacity of his court. . . . He
could see his boy grow up the Son of

* From Robert Sencourt, *Napoleon III: The Modern Emperor.* Copyright, 1933 by
Ernest Benn Limited. Reprinted by permission.

France, and see his collection of the wonders of the world admired by sovereign after sovereign, and each of them his guests in the Tuileries and on the Champ de Mars. He could see the great of Europe gathered at his dinners, and his jewelled Empress, as she turned, throw down the table the sparkle of her glance.

He could see other scenes: Donna Virginia Castiglione in her cambric nightgown at Compiègne, the sweet eyes, the blooming presence of Lady Mary Craven, the curls and bosom of Madame de Mercy-Argenteau as, at the end of the underground passage into the Elysée, she sank into his arms.

He might have thought of solider things—of the order he had given to France, the railways completed, the production and commerce increased, the well-being of the people, the disappearance of unemployment, the free trade with England which had fed the people, the clearing, beautifying, rebuilding of Paris, the reservation of the Bois, the trees in the Champs Elysées, the sward of the Parc Monceau, the central arteries of traffic. He might have thought of the changes in Italy which he had made, and the Alpine frontier which he had secured against the great new country; of the steadfast alliance that he had maintained with England; of the new independence of Rumania which he had encouraged. Even the rise of Prussia and the unification of Germany he had championed, though they brought his fall.

He might have looked into the future, and seen that fall avenged, and his Empress there to see; he might have seen an older fancy realized: the Austrian dominions broken up: the Ottoman Empire shrinking out of Europe. Poland and Rumania emerging as strong nations;

the Vatican making her settlement with Italy almost on the precise lines that he had so insistently commended; Russia, crashing as he had foreseen, because there was nothing of his own ideals in her system. All that was to come. He was to be the Modern Napoleon—the man who by his work made, and prepared for, the Europe of which the founder of his dynasty had dreamed. For this we see to have been his fate: to have been the man of a time two generations later than his own: of a time which alike in its love of comfort, in its loose conscience as to the relations of men and women, in its taste for tobacco, for diversion, for careless spending, and international congresses, in its mingling of light pleasures with humanitarian generosities, in its ever present sense of the problems of unemployment, of communism, of the well-being of the workman: a time which in these things has trended back from a belief in parliamentary government to a dependence on dictators like himself. That is his significance: not to be recognized, not to be comprehensible, but in the light of what was done by the men who were young when he, more than any was the guiding, the prophetic mind of France and Europe.... Disease gradually robbed him of the power hidden in the reactions of his temperament—the power which Lytton diagnosed and which Victoria understood—but even in his weakness and his mistakes, he, as a Bonaparte, proved that there was in him, as in his more famous predecessor, an elasticity, a resilience, which make him a power when he seemed to have left the world branded as a failure. He completed the career of Napoleon I. Who has completed his own?

Even in the age which fulfils so many

of his prophecies, and brings into the world of fact so many of his dreams, his memorable sayings have a cogency that is far from being exhausted. Even when his Empress saw his cause triumph, she might have noted that victorious France and victorious England seemed to have forgotten what Napoleon III never forgot, to be generous to his enemies, and to seek the welfare of their people. During the Crimean War he had Russian products at his Exhibition; at the end of the Austrian War, he had fallen in love with the Austrian Emperor. But, at Versailles in 1919, it was Bismarck's psychology which ruled, not that of Napoleon III. Clémenceau and English Conservatives were still insisting that the screw of starvation should be put on women and children rather than negotiate for a sane and enduring peace. Was France still to find her example in Bismarck? Had Germany nothing to learn from Napoleon III?

Let us remember still that he never tried to disturb the economic unity, the *Zollverein,* of Germany: still less did he ever dream of disturbing that of Austria-Hungary. In all his ambition for Poland, he never spoke of anything so ancient and provocative as giving her a corridor through Prussia. Though a partisan of nationality for Germany, for Italy, for Rumania, for Hungary, he maintained the ideal of concord, of peace, of unity among all nations. "It is civil war to fight in Europe," he loved to repeat. "The time for conquests is over," he said again. "I long for the time when the great questions which divide Governments and peoples can be settled peacefully by European arbitration... Let our only thought of obstacles be to overcome them, and of incredulity to confound it."

And his European ideal is no less cogent to-day than the social one which he was already promulgating a hundred years ago:

To admit any saving that without disorganizing the public service will allow the reduction of the taxes that press the hardest on the people, to encourage undertakings, which, by developing agriculture give work to those that want it; to provide for the old age of workingmen by establishing benefit societies: to introduce into our legislation modifications tending not to ruin the rich for the benefit of the poor, but to base the prosperity of each in that of all: to restrain within proper limits the employment which depends on the State: to avoid the shameful tendency which leads the State to undertake works which private enterprise can do better....

Nor was it his habit to trust to any mechanical scheme either political or economic. He tried to remove the restrictions which hinder private enterprise. And to strengthen the same motive which gives the man with power and privilege a sense of his responsibilities, and to the poor their patience and their hope, he consistently encouraged religion, supporting the Church which was the most powerful spiritual instrument in France and in Europe, but also showing every courtesy and consideration to other denominations. He was not a theologian, probably not even a believer, but he looked towards heaven for a charity which men without the graces of an interior life too often allow their selfishness to stifle.

There are some men to whom one can look for theories and ideals more valuable than they attained in practice. So it is with this mixed man whose weaknesses are too gross to extenuate: but in France, as in Germany, such weaknesses are common ones, never regarded as monstrous. Looking indeed at Napoleon III—

You
Shall find there a man, who is the abstracts of all faults
That all men follow.

For at least five and forty years it was his habit "to fill his vacancy with his voluptuousness." But if he had the fault of Mark Anthony, he had also much of the generosity, some of the grandeur....

...And if his political importance was rather in the sense that he was a Rabbi ben Ezra, with projects nobler than his accomplishments, and also another Hernani, an agent of the forces round him, rather than their master, yet it must be remembered that his significance for the future was always bound up with definite principles actively exerted, with a dictatorial power maintained for more than twenty years and singularly fruitful, and with a gift to win and hold the hearts of men. "As long as I live I must regret him," wrote the Queen of Holland when she heard of his death. "It was impossible to know him in his intimacy without admiring and loving his patience, gentleness, unselfishness."

He was far from being a hero. He was still further from being a saint. He was one of those whose taste for intrigue convinces them that the end justifies the means. We must not forget that, at the instigation of Cavour, he for Italy, played many of the tricks which in the case of Bismarck were afterwards turned against him. But he remained for those among whom he lived both solicitous and lovable. It was not only his mistresses who were his admirers. Both his mother and his son adored him, and his wife, at the end, wrote that there was something in his gentleness which made her think of Christ. There is much in this which can be explained only by his personal magnetism. Behind that magnetism nevertheless was also a warm and deep benevolence: a regard not only for his people, and his country, but also for Europe, if not for the world.... He was generous to his enemies: he was always faithful to those who had befriended him. Among his courtiers, there was not one but loved him; long after his death the peasants remembered his reign as a golden age, and the veterans of his defeated army, when they heard his name, felt a straining at their hearts, and the tears started to their eyes, so warm was their devotion to him who, with all his oddness, all his failings, all his contrasts, and all his surprises, was not quite unworthy to be the last, for he was also, both in will and deed, the kindest of their Sovereigns.

In a book written a few years after World War II, J. SALWYN SCHAPIRO (1879–   ), Professor Emeritus of the City College of New York, an authority on eighteenth- and nineteenth-century liberalism, discusses Louis Napoleon under the general heading: "Heralds of Fascism." Here, by throwing "the light of the present on the past," the author links Louis Napoleon and twentieth-century fascism; this was the first emphatic analysis by a respected scholar to suggest that fascism might be an outgrowth of the Second Empire. The indictment came as a surprise to many historians, but now the general thesis is so widely known that virtually every writer on the Second Empire must take it into account.*

► # *Louis Napoleon Bonaparte, Statesman*

Far more significant than the revival of clericalism was the revival of Bonapartism, in a new social setting with a political program, the significance of which has become clear only in our day. Into the new revolutionary situation created by socialism came the enigmatic figure of Louis Napoleon Bonaparte (1808–1873). . . .

After the February Revolution in 1848 Louis Napoleon came prominently to the fore. His name, his romantic experiences, his appeals to the glorious memories of the First Empire made him a popular figure. After the upheaval of the "June Days," Louis Napoleon appealed to many as the "savior of society," the strong "man on horseback" who

would suppress the socialist terror as Napoleon I had suppressed the Jacobin terror. Nothing could be more ridiculous than the pose of Louis Napoleon as the embodiment of the "Napoleonic legend." The weak-chinned, short-legged, rouged "man on horseback" of 1848 was hardly even a caricature of the great Napoleon. The cynical French were not at all deceived by the romantic propaganda of the Bonapartist party. Louis Napoleon's appeal had a far more solid basis in that the propertied classes saw in him a powerful force able and willing to make use of a dictatorial government to save them from social revolution. He gained the solid support of all who feared a social revolution: property owners great and small, aristocrats, capitalists, peasant proprietors, shopkeepers, and professionals; Catholics who dreaded a revival of attacks on the church by a socialist Reign of Terror; and people generally, who recoiled with horror at the prospect of class war. Barely a year after the February Revolution, the generous glow of democracy and republicanism gave way to a hardened resolve to establish a political system that would be neither democratic nor republican.

Wherein lay the appeal of Louis Napoleon as the "savior of society"? Nothing in his expressed views marked him as a conservative defender of vested interests and of class privileges. On the contrary, he had severely criticized capitalism and had asserted that his chief desire was to promote the welfare of the workers. Early in his career, Louis Napoleon had written three books ... in which he presented his views on the reconstruction of France. These writings breathed the atmosphere of Utopian socialism of the first half of the nineteenth century. Louis Napoleon's early associations were with the disciples of Charles Fourier and of Saint-Simon; he was an intimate of Louis Blanc; and he was sufficiently interested in Proudhon to have an extended discussion with him on social problems.

Louis Napoleon endorsed the socialist view that capitalism was a new feudalism imposed on mankind. "Property in land," he declared, "had its vassals and its serfs. The revolution enfranchised the land; but the new property—that of the manufacturers—growing daily, tended ... to have, like the first, its vassals and its serfs. He denounced the industrial system, which, he asserted, was responsible for starvation amidst plenty. It was the disgrace of the nineteenth century that "a tenth part of our population is in rags, and dying from starva-

tion, when there are millions of francs' worth of manufactured produce which cannot find a sale, and millions of the productions of the earth which cannot be consumed." To create better conditions, Louis Napoleon advocated the establishment of cooperative agricultural colonies on unused land, to be financed by government loans. This reform would absorb the unemployed and raise the standard of living for millions. In this manner, he argued, prosperity would come to the entire nation. ...

Along with denunciation of capitalism and with concern for the workers' welfare, an anti-Semitic note was sounded by the supporters of Louis Napoleon, when he became a candidate for the presidency of the Republic. Louis Napoleon they asserted, was the true socialist, who would destroy the "antisocial combination of cosmopolitan capitalists," such as the Jewish bankers, the Rothschilds, by abolishing their financial privileges. A Bonapartist journal, *Organisation du travail,* was established, "in the interest of democracy and of the proletariat," to exorcise the evil influence of Jewish finance in France. Another Bonapartist journal, *Napoléon républicain,* held the Jews responsible for the disasters suffered by France during the First Empire and for the defeat of Napoleon I. "The infamous financiers of the period, with the Jew Rothschild at their head," retarded the Emperor's campaign in Russia through their manipulations. That was the true cause of the Emperor's collapse. This interpretation of the fall of the First Empire has the familiar sound of the "stab in the back" by the Jews, popularized by Hitler to explain the downfall of the German Empire. Black lists appeared, bearing the names of bankers who, it was charged, became rich by robbing the people. Most of the names on the black lists were those of Jews and of foreigners, who were denounced as being responsible for all the evils in France.

During the presidential campaign in 1848 the supporters of Louis Napoleon appealed to the workers to vote for him as the man who was both a democrat and a socialist. The success of Louis Napoleon's candidacy was so overwhelming that his appeal to the radical workers could not have been unheeded. Not a few of them, discouraged by the suppression of the uprising in the "June Days," rallied to Louis Napoleon as a better choice than his bourgeois opponents. Socialism without terror was attractive to many radicals, who were convinced that Louis Napoleon would perform where the socialists had promised so hopefully and had failed so tragically in the fateful year 1848. There is no keener interpreter of the situation in France during the Revolution of 1848 than Proudhon. "Everywhere," he wrote, in 1848, "the socialist instinct and the deepest republicanism found themselves united by the name 'Napoleon,' who was and still is to the masses the Revolution incarnate."

The struggle between the Assembly and the President, during the period 1848 to 1851, has been generally interpreted as that between a democratic Republic fighting for its life and an adventurer aiming to become a military dictator. Obviously that was not true; the Assembly, controlled by a royalist majority, had taken the first step to abolish the Republic by destroying its foundation—manhood suffrage. The real issue between the Assembly and the President was what method was to be used in order to allay the fears caused by the "June Days." The method offered by the Assembly was the old one, namely, a return to monarchy buttressed by clericalism....What was needed was a new pattern of resistance to revolution. That was furnished by Louis Napoleon. His method to fight the revolutionary socialists, then as now called "communists," was by establishing a dictatorship, organized on a popular basis and committed to a program of social reform. "Now the reign of castes is over," declared Louis Napoleon, "multitudes are to be governed; they must therefore be organized that they may express their wishes, and be disciplined that they may be directed and enlightened for their own advantage." This new type of dictatorial government would be able to defend property rights and to suppress revolutionaries with a vigor that neither the Bourbons nor Louis Philippe could exercise because they lacked the all-essential popular support. To conciliate the embittered workers and, at the same time, to quiet the fears of the propertied classes was the new political pattern presented by Louis Napoleon.

The overthrow of the Second Republic by the *coup d'état* of December 2, 1851, was the necessary and inevitable outcome of the election of Louis Napoleon to the presidency. And the proclamation of the Second Empire, which shortly followed the *coup d'état,* completed the strange, yet expected, turn of events in France. If the suppression of the Second Republic was the result of a conspiracy, it was an open conspiracy. No one was really surprised, as the *coup d'état* was ratified by a vote of 7,439,216 to 646,737. "The defeat of socialist democracy," observed Proudhon, "first in 1848 and 1849, and then in 1851 and 1852, is the very pivot of our present history.... The danger of socialism brings to the support of the Empire the united forces of the conflicting groups now out of power: the Legitimists, the Orleanists, the moderate Republicans, and the Catholics."

Like that of 1799, the *coup d'état* of 1851 was a revolutionary antidote to the revolutionary tradition in France. It was a desperate device born of the need to protect a social order established by one revolution from being overthrown by another. For this reason, the regime of Napoleon III was under the continuous necessity of proclaiming democratic ideals and of maintaining at least the appearance of democratic methods through plebiscites and elections. A naked autocracy, based on sheer despotism, could not have restrained for long the revolutionary forces in the nation.

The Second Empire was no more a restoration of the First Empire than the rule of the Bourbons, after 1815, was a restoration of the Old Regime. Despite the trappings and fittings of its Napoleonic predecessor, with which the Second Empire adorned itself, its advent marked the appearance of something new in political systems and in political ideologies. The real significance of the Second Empire is greater today than when it flourished. The methods that it employed, the policies that it pursued, and the ideas that it proclaimed anticipated in a vague, incomplete way what is now known as "fascism." Like fascism, it arose from similar conditions. During the reign of Louis Philippe the Industrial Revolution ... in France advanced rapidly enough to throw many out of work, but not rapidly enough to absorb them into the new industries. As a consequence, there was "an overwhelming mass of people without a career and a young generation without a future. ... This was the chief reason for the constantly recurring agitations, the infinite source of public and private suffering."

Two generations later there was a historic parallel to the overthrow of the Second French Republic. In Italy, after the First World War, a dangerous situation was created by the economic disorganization that followed the end of hostilities. There was widespread unemployment and the government did little to alleviate the evil conditions under which millions were suffering. Deep resentment among the Italian workers led them to give a ready ear to those who preached social revolution: socialists, syndicalists, and communists. The revolutionary temper of the embittered workers reached the boiling point in 1920, when they went on a general strike and seized the factories. Though the uprising quickly collapsed, there was great apprehension among the propertied classes, who feared that the seizure of the factories was but a rehearsal for a socialist revolution. And they consequently gave their powerful support to the movement, led by Mussolini, to establish a fascist dictatorship. France in 1848 strikingly resembled Italy in 1920. Fear that the "June Days" were but a rehearsal for a socialist revolution had impelled the propertied classes in France to rally behind Napoleon. Mussolini's March on Rome in 1922 paralleled Napoleon's *coup d'état* in 1851.

Like Mussolini, Napoleon puzzled and confused many of his contemporaries. Even the usually perspicacious and farsighted De Tocqueville had no inkling of the real significance of Napoleon, of whom he held no high opinion. According to De Tocqueville, Napoleon's "intelligence was incoherent, confused, filled with great but ill-assorted thoughts, which he borrowed now from the examples of Napoleon, now from socialist theories, sometimes from recollections of England, where he lived: very different, and often very contrary, sources." He was "naturally a dreamer and a visionary." And one could not be long in contact with him "without discovering a little vein of madness which was chiefly responsible for his success." The powerful interests that, openly or secretly, rallied to Napoleon's support had no great opinion of his ability or confidence in the strength of his character. What they wanted him to do was to eliminate the socialists from the political scene with a strong hand and then to become their pliant tool in the government of France.... Once in power, Napoleon swept aside the bourgeois politicians as ruthlessly as he suppressed the socialist revolutionists.

Nothing is easier than to find factual parallels in history. They are generally plausible, seldom convincing, and never instructive. To see the origins of great changes in history is a quite different— and more important—matter. As nature abhors a vacuum, history abhors changes without origins, whether immediate or remote. Fascism did not spring fully grown from the chin of Mussolini. It had historic origins, not so much in Italy itself as in France, which since the French Revolution has furnished many revolutionary patterns to Latin Europe.

The organization and policies of the Second Empire bore startling resemblances to the fascist dictatorships of our time. It was a dictatorship based on popular support, as expressed in plebiscites and in "elections." Napoleon realized what neither the Bourbons nor Louis Philippe had realized: that popular support was all essential in maintaining a government in post-revolutionary France. To obtain popular support he established a parliament, the *Corps législatif*, elected by manhood suffrage. The acid test of parliamentary government is the existence of an opposition that arises from free elections and that aims to assume power. No parliamentary opposition existed throughout the period of the Second Empire. The method of "official candidates," already established by the Bourbons and perfected into a system by the July Monarchy, concerned a small electorate, which was easily controlled. Under the Second Empire this system was applied thoroughly and efficiently to the huge electorate that came with manhood suffrage, punctiliously maintained by Napoleon. Official candidates were put in nomination in every district by a smoothly running political machine, organized by the government. For a time few, if any, opposition candidates appeared. Under the Second Empire there was a false majority in parliament, elected by manhood suffrage, as there had been false majorities in the parliaments of the Bourbon and Orleanist monarchies, which had been elected by small groups of property owners. As in the fascist dictatorships, the voters under the Second Empire went to the polls, not to elect representatives, but to endorse the list of candidates drawn up by the government; and parliament met not to pass laws but to ratify decrees presented by the government. In fact, though not in theory, elections were conducted on a one-party basis. It took a bold and courageous man to oppose the official candidate; an opposition candidate at the elections was sure to arouse the vindictive enmity of the government. Few dared to assume such a risk. In 1857 the government presented for reelection all the members of the outgoing parliament. This complete flouting of the democratic process created widespread resentment which found expression in the election of five opposition candidates. *Les cinq*, as the opponents of the government were known, constituted the beginning of a parliamentary opposition, which grew in numbers during the last decade of the Second Empire.

Public opinion in France, as expressed in the press, was traditionally antigovernment. Napoleon conceived the idea of having the entire press used as the mouthpiece of the government, an idea later applied in the fascist dictatorships. A highly organized censorship controlled, cajoled, directed, or terrorized the newspapers into becoming organs of the government. Opposition newspapers were suppressed and their editors jailed or exiled. Suppression of opposition newspapers was not a new thing in post-revolutionary France. What was new was the systematic use of the entire press to give the illusion that public opinion supported the government. Like manhood suffrage, the press was an integral part of the new type of dictatorship, which boasted of being the expression of the popular will.

What did the "socialist Emperor" do about labor? To allay the bourgeois terror of a class struggle between labor and capital, trade-unions were outlawed and strikes forbidden. In 1853 the government inaugurated a method of labor-capital cooperation through a system of industrial councils representing both sides. To these councils, *conseils des prud'hommes,* was given the task of regulating wages, hours, and conditions in the factories. Such bodies had existed before, but under the Second Empire they were used by the government to support its labor policies. Frequently men not even connected with the industry were appointed by the authorities as officials of the *conseils.* As a system, the *conseils* suggested the Nazi Labor Front, in that they were intermediary

groups between the workers and the government, under the political direction of the latter and used as a means of controlling the former. What the Emperor desired, writes a latter-day apologist of Napoleon, was "to create an army of workers of the same type as that created by the National Socialists in German a century later."

Another way of controlling the workers was through the *livret.* In 1854 a law made more stringent the regulations of this industrial pass-port in order to enable the police to keep watch over the comings and goings of the workers. Since the "June Days" there was a great dread of the Paris worker, who was regarded as the uncompromising enemy of the social order, ever ready to overthrow it by mass insurrection. A secret report on the attitude of the working class, made by a government agent, asserted that the worker was a socialist as, before 1789, the bourgeois had been a *philosophe.* "The bourgeois sought to establish a system that they could use as a weapon against the dominance of the nobility and the clergy. The worker now favors a system which he can use to overthrow, if possible, all inequalities." During the Second Empire the workers, cowed by repressive measures, were silent, industrious, and, to all appearances, submissive. Despite the great advance of industry during the regime of Napoleon, the condition of the mass of workers did not improve greatly. It was estimated that there were then in France about three million paupers and about six million who were often in a condition below the poverty line.

What did Napoleon do to advance social reform, which had been the burden of his appeal to the workers? Very little. He did nothing at all to establish the agricultural colonies that he had advocated so fervently in his *De l'extinction du paupérisme.* Government subventions were given to associations having for their object old-age pensions and sickness insurance. To diminish unemployment, the government instituted *les grands travaux,* public works of which the rebuilding of Paris was the most famous project. The social reforms of the Second Empire were meager performances, considering the generous promises that the Emperor had made when he was bidding for power.

The class that benefited most from the Second Empire was the *bourgeoisie.* Napoleon had learned from his early associates, the disciples of Saint-Simon, that a new historic era had come with the Industrial Revolution. Thenceforth, the capitalists, not the aristocrats, were to be the ruling class in society. The chief aim of the Saint-Simonians was the economic development of France. They were little interested in political rights and in popular government, and generally subordinated political to economic questions. If any intellectual group could be said to have been the mentors of the Second Empire, it was the Saint-Simonians. Closely associated with the government in its various economic enterprises were Michel Chevalier, the brothers Pereire, and Pere Enfantin—all disciples of the famous Utopian socialist.

Napoleon did all in his power to encourage commerce and industry, which won for the government the powerful support of the new moneyed class. Anti-Semitism played no part in the Emperor's policies, despite its upflare during his campaign for the presidency; the Jewish bankers, the Rothschild family and the brothers Pereire, were very influential in government finance. The pace of industrialization in France after 1815 had been slow, hampered in part by aristocratic indifference, in part by socialist agitation. During the Second Empire, France was in a fever of business enterprise and machine production. Two new financial institutions, the *Crédit foncier* and the *Crédit mobilier,* financed the building of the great railway system of France, the rebuilding of Paris, and the organization of the French Line operating trans-Atlantic steamships. Railway mileage increased six-fold during the period of the Second Empire. Steel production was greatly increased by the expansion of the steel plant at Le Creusot. The horsepower of machines used in industry quintupled. France was beginning to catch up with England in the rapid development of modern industry.

In his economic as well as in his political policies, reconciliation was the watchword of Napoleon III. He desired to reconcile capital with labor; authoritative government with manhood suffrage; and a rigid censorship with a free press. The prime motive of his reconciliation policy was to solve the as yet unsolved problem of the two Frances. Napoleon fully realized the vital importance of the problem, as well as the failure of the different political groups to solve it.... He came to the conclusion that all efforts to bring unity to France had failed because they had all been partisan in character: Legitimist, bourgeois liberal, or republican. Because he belonged to none of these parties, insisted Napoleon, he was best fitted to unite the two Frances. He would do so by a plan that incorporated the fundamental principle of each political element. From the Legitimists he would take the monarchical principle, by establishing a new dynasty. From the bourgeois liberals he would take the parliamentary principle, by establishing a representative body. From the republicans he would take the principle of popular sovereignty, by maintaining manhood suffrage. He would reassure the propertied classes by suppressing socialist revolts. To reassure the workers, "Saint-Simon on horseback," as Napoleon was called, would institute social reforms for the welfare of the masses. This uniting of the various conflicting elements would *terminer enfin la Révolution française,* and the two Frances at last would become one.

There was to be a guarantee of this unity: authoritarian government. The dictatorial rule of Napoleon was carried out with great firmness. Thousands of recalcitrant republicans were exiled or imprisoned or were compelled to flee. ...The Legitimists and the Orleanists, less recalcitrant, were ignored. The church was cajoled into supporting the regime by the *loi Falloux* and by the encouragement given to the clergy.... Though the regime of the Second Empire was not "totalitarian" in the fascist sense, almost every institution in the land felt the hand of the government, which regulated, prescribed, punished, and suppressed opinions and activities that were hostile to Napoleon.

Did the Napoleonic dictatorship succeed in solving the persistent problem of uniting the two Frances? It certainly seemed so. All through the period of the Second Empire domestic peace reigned in France; no uprisings, no strikes of any consequence, and no serious parliamentary opposition disquieted the government. The nation appeared to be united behind the Emperor, who, toward the end of his reign, received an almost unanimous vote of confidence as a result

of a plebiscite. But appearances belied the realities of the situation in France. On the morrow of the fall of the Empire there broke out the bloodiest uprising in the revolutionary history of France—the Paris Commune Dictatorship had not been a solution.

In an extraordinary, penetrating pamphlet, *De l'esprit de conquête et de l'usurpation,* Benjamin Constant gave an analysis of the methods used by a dictator in ruling a nation. What he said referred to Napoleon I, but it applied even more forcefully to the methods used by Napoleon III. "The existence of public sentiment," he wrote, "being dangerous to dictatorship and the semblance of public sentiment being necessary to it, the dictatorship strikes the people with one hand to stifle any real sentiment; and it strikes them again with the other hand to compel them to act as if motivated by public sentiment." When a dictator "condemns innocence, he includes calumny so that his action will seem to be justified." When he decides on a policy, the dictator orders "a ridiculous investigation to serve as a prelude to what he had decided to do. This counterfeit liberty combines all the evils of anarchy and slavery. There is no end to a tyranny which seeks to drag forth tokens of consent. Peaceable men are persecuted for indifference, energetic men, for being dangerous." Dictatorship invents a falsified popular approval of the government; and the result is that fear "comes to ape all the appearances of courage, to congratulate itself on dishonor, and to give thanks for unhappiness." Dictatorship resorts to the practice of hiring corrupt journalists who parody freedom of the press. They "argue, as though trying to convince; they fly into a passion as though fighting an opposition; they fling insults

as though there was any chance of re-
plying." Under a despotic monarchy,
the people are enslaved; but under a
dictatorship, they are also degraded. A
dictatorship "debases a people while op-
pressing them, and accustoms them to
trample under foot what they once
respected, to court what they once
scorned, and even to scorn themselves."

Nazi writers in Germany have evalu-
ated the historic importance of Napoleon as a harbinger of fascism, despite
the marked differences between the Second Empire and the Third Reich. A
book, *Masse oder Volk,* written by Kon-
stantin Frantz in 1852, was republished
in 1933 with a significant preface by
the Nazi Franz Kemper. "The rise to
power of Louis Napoleon," wrote Kemper, "is the only historical parallel to
the National Socialist revolution of our
day." According to Frantz, the Napoleonic state depended on mass support,
without which it could not be maintained even by the powerful Imperial
army. Only through social reform could
the danger of socialism be eliminated.
In the view of another Nazi writer,
Michael Freund, Napoleon was the only
real revolutionist in 1848. "After the
solemn republican respectability of 1848
it seemed that only with the Napoleonic
experiment did a great revolutionary
elan appear on the stage of history."
The state created by Napoleon was anti-
socialist, but it was not the laissez-faire
state of capitalism. The social ideals of
the disciples of Saint-Simon were given
by Napoleon, for the first time, a military
and authoritarian aspect. Still another
Nazi, K. H. Bremer, diagnosed the situation of the Second Republic in the
following manner. While the republicans of 1848 were trying to solve the
constitutional question, he observed, Napoleon realized that the social question
was the most important one. Parlia-

mentarism, with its conflicting political
parties and class struggles, was incapable
of solving the social question. Only a
dictatorship with a social outlook, in the
view of Napoleon, could solve it. His
great aim was to establish a political
system based upon the unity of all
classes and of all interests in France. It
was he, according to Bremer, who first
created the new type of state in the
form of authoritarian, plebiscitarian
leadership.

The prefascist pattern of Napoleon's
dictatorship collapsed even before Sedan.
What was called the "Liberal Empire,"
inaugurated in 1867, marked a definite
trend toward liberalism. Elections became freer, and opposition parties appeared in parliament. The control of
the press was relaxed. Public meetings
were more freely permitted. Even more
significant were the concessions made to
the workers. Trade-unions were legal-
ized, collective bargaining was recognized, and strikes were permitted.

What caused this transition from the
fascist pattern of the dictatorship to
the pattern of the "Liberal Empire"?
Rising discontent among powerful elements in the nation forced Napoleon to
make concessions to liberalism. The
protectionists opposed his reciprocity
treaty with England. The Catholics opposed his alliance with the Italian
nationalists in the Austro-Sardinian war.
The liberals loudly demanded a return
to constitutional government and the
restoration of "the necessary liberties."
The disastrous failure of the Emperor's
intervention in Mexico brought the dis-
contented elements together in a common hostility to the Empire. Napoleon
sought to ward off by timely concessions
a revolutionary upheaval such as had
overtaken his predecessor, Louis Philippe; hence, *l'Empire libéral.*

These   explanations,   while   true

enough, merely indicate the weakness of the Second Empire as a fascist experiment. Neither Hitler nor Mussolini made any concessions to liberalism throughout their dictatorships. *The weakness of the fascist pattern of Napoleon lay in that it did not include totalitarianism.* Napoleon never attempted "to coordinate" the political, economic, and social life of France into a uniform, unified, national system, run by a dictatorial machine. He would not have succeeded had he tried to do so. There were serious obstacles to totalitarianism in the France of his day. Despite fairly rapid industrial advance during the Second Empire, France continued to be primarily an agricultural nation. Land was cultivated by millions of peasant proprietors, passionately individualistic, who would quickly have resented any abrogation of their rights as independent cultivators. There did not then exist large combinations of basic industries, which easily lend themselves to government control and regulation. French industry generally was based on small competitive units that could not be "coordinated" even by the most despotic of dictatorships. Neither was there a large working class, organized in powerful trade-unions, that could be taken over and directed by a dictatorship. Totalitarianism requires, in addition, easy and rapid means of communication and transportation, such as radio, motion pictures, automobiles, and airplanes, which a dictatorship can use for propaganda purposes. It also requires a national school system in which the masses of the people can be indoctrinated with a common ideology. France of the mid-nineteenth century had none of these means of "coordination." Had Napoleon attempted to do what Hitler did so quickly and so successfully, the revolutionary tocsin would have been heard in every hamlet and in every quarter of France.

The social experiment of the dictatorship of Napoleon is the most significant aspect of the Second Empire. It has been obscured by the sensational foreign policies of the Emperor, which led to the Crimean, the Austro-Sardinian, and the Franco-Prussian wars, and finally to his dramatic downfall. In the light of fascism, it can now be discerned that a new political method of fighting social revolution had been devised, namely, to turn the revolutionary stream of working-class discontent into the new channel of a popular and socialized dictatorship. Napoleon's pioneer fascism failed, and its failure discredited the newly born legend of "Saint-Simon on horseback." It also discredited militarism, with which the experiment was so closely linked. The downfall of the Second Empire exploded the "Napoleonic legend" so violently that even Napoleon I was struck by the flying missiles. The great Napoleon, as well as Napoleon-le-petit, now appeared to the French as an "architect of ruin." Waterloo and Sedan became joined, in popular opinion, as the outstanding national disasters in the history of France.

Strangely enough, bourgeois liberalism also was discredited by the Second Empire. The social experiments of Napoleon, however tentative and halting, and the maintenance of manhood suffrage, however, illusory and ineffective, yet kept alive a democratic sentiment in France. A restoration of bourgeois liberalism, with its neglect of the working class and with its capitalist rule, was as distasteful after 1870 as the restoration of the Bourbons had been after 1815. If it did nothing else, the Second Empire had accustomed the French people to think of government in its intimate relationship with their everyday problems.

In the next selection we leave general over-all characterizations of Napoleon III and examine a specific administrative organ of his empire, the political police. HOWARD C. PAYNE (1916–   ) of the State University of Washington, a specialist in the periods of the Second Empire and Third Republic, presents by inference a partial response to Schapiro. Omitted is a portion of the article that explores the theoretical foundations of the political police. Finding its power "virtually unlimited in theory," Payne then delineates its practical operation under the Second Empire.*

Political Police during the Second Empire

Many of the post-December prefects saw in the new regime an administrative Valhalla, a new freedom to realize their "administrative independence" to the limits of political police theory. Their reports and instructions enunciated a veritable "ideology" of political police, overlaid by the Bonapartist mystique of plebiscitary dictatorship.... After December 1851 it was only necessary to develop the theory and practice of political police within the old ideological and institutional setting, altered so as to impose fewer restraints on familiar police activities. Indeed, the coup of 1851 was but the climax of a two-year "creeping coup d'état," wherein all political police powers were mobilized and enlisted in Louis-Napoleon's cause.

The act of December 2 did, however, open a brief period of arbitrary and extraordinary police powers ruthlessly used.... Prefects were told to ignore due process of law in political cases, on the pragmatic grounds that "the court debates ensuing from an application of common law would constitute a new public danger...."

Extraordinary powers ceased on March 27, 1852.... Presumably political police would subside into habitual channels. And so it did—except that the channels

* From Howard C. Payne, "Theory and Practice of Political Police during the Second Empire in France," *Journal of Modern History,* XXX, no. 1 (March 1958). Copyright 1958 by the University of Chicago. Used by permission of the University of Chicago Press.

were broadened by the Constitution of 1852 and certain legislation intended to facilitate the political mission of the police.

... New laws did not so much define new political offenses as increase administrative prerogative at the expense of the courts.... The commonest political charges in press cases stemmed from legislation anterior to the Second Empire. Armed with past legislation and present increments in administrative authority, the political police after 1852 controlled the press with less recourse either to warnings or prosecutions. Unofficial pressure—methods, termed *officieux* not *officiels*—increasingly sufficed until the relaxing of press controls in the 1860's. Press prosecutions between 1852 and 1861 were fewer than during the July Monarchy and Second Republic.

New legislation on associations and public reunions likewise merely "codified" earlier restrictions and increased prefectorial latitude in enforcement.... The decree of December 8, 1851, perhaps the most notorious special legislation, allowed certain categories of political offenders or suspects to be transported or put under rigid police surveillance by administrative decision....

... A series of "decentralization" decrees between 1852 and 1867 actually added to centralized police controls by giving prefects more discretion in on-the-spot decisions and appointments of local police personnel, all under the close scrutiny of the minister of the interior. Prefects welcomed such augmentation of political police power as a more fitting and adequate realization of "administrative independence."

The emperor and successive ministers of the interior sought greater technical efficiency by experiments in the reorganization of police services. Certain of these essays were frustrated; others had lasting effects on the French police. The most radical of these was the abortive ministry of general police, which lasted from January 1852 to June 1853. Desiring at once a revival of Napoleonic tradition and a more complete embodiment of political police theory, De Maupas, minister of police, built a super-hierarchy of political police officials over the existing structure. He found that 1852 was a long way from 1799! By 1852 administrative agents had evolved a sense of corporate interests which they saw threatened by the ministry of police.... Having virtually "made" the coup d'etat for Louis-Napoleon in order to assure government by administration, the prefects (aided by their minister, De Persigny) now un-made the ministry of general police for the same reason. "Administrative independence" had more than one meaning for Napoleon III....

More comprehensive police centralization was achieved by the creation of the *Sûreté publique* in 1859. By this reform the Paris prefect of police received general (and hence political) police jurisdiction over the whole of France, assuming many police powers and responsibilities formerly lodged in the ministry of the interior. Prefects whose own status was unaffected by the change now had at their disposal the resources of the Parisian police administration, including some 3,500,000 personal dossiers....

The emperor's most successful and subtle innovation was his use of the *Gendarmerie.* The 24,000 *gendarmes* were part of the army but, being placed in small *brigades* throughout France, were at the prefects' disposal for police duties, political and otherwise.... As early as

November 1849, the *Gendarmerie* had "very confidential" instructions to undertake "an entirely new" political mission on behalf of Louis-Napoleon, who thus developed a tacit "alliance" with the corps, increasing its pay and personnel before and after the coup d'etat. *Gendarmes* loyally aided the coup . . . . . . the emperor received direct, confidential political police summaries, including reports on other police agencies. . . . Prefects, ministers of interior, and Parisian prefects of police were often jealously suspicious of the *Gendarmerie's* political role and resentful of its proud *esprit de corps;* but most prefects attested to the value of their services as political police in the countryside. . . .

Although most political police work was part of administrative routine, certain aspects were necessarily confidential or secret. . . . The study of the secret police is a major problem in itself, but some tentative conclusions may be offered. Materials for the study of secret police methods, despite the much-publicized loss of Parisian records, are available . . . and they are particularly plentiful in some departmental archives. Examination of some of these for the years 1849 to 1869 shows no impressive change in secret police work in 1852 or later, either in kind or in quantity. Contrary to estimates of secret police funds rising as high as 14,000,000 francs yearly, the archives show an average of somewhat over 2,000,000 francs annually, except in 1858 (3,200,000). These sums were not significantly larger than those spent in earlier regimes (since 1828), and less than the secret funds expended in 1848. Many prefects complained of the inadequacy of secret funds and secret agents, often protesting against actual cuts in their customary allotments.

Secret agents were most used to infiltrate and inform on workers' organizations and secret political societies. . . . most police spies were volunteers or members of secret societies who informed because of police pressure or persuasion. *Provocateurs* were used, but the evidence suggests that more conspiracies against emperor and government were genuine than historians usually assume, though their magnitude was often exaggerated by the police. Outside Paris, the main centers of the secret police were in Marseille and Lyon. It seems likely that the invidious role attributed to the secret police by contemporaries of the Second Empire reflected a reaction against the general emphasis upon political police which accompanied the dictatorship rather than a tremendous increase of secret police.

Certain restraints kept the police from realizing their potentialities or the hopes of the most authoritarian leaders of the regime. One kind of restraint, already cited . . . was the corporate resistance of the prefectorial bureaucracy. . . . The judiciary offered another obstacle to administration power by insisting, within their own jurisdiction, upon acceptable evidence, due process of law, and the autonomy of justice. Often the judiciary were more Orleanist than Bonapartist, or at least impervious to Napoleonic "ideology," and were inclined to withhold the degree of co-operation expected by police authorities.

Incompetence and lack of initiative . . . were the subject of frequent complaints by the higher officials. The rank and file, and some higher officials, were not systematically trained or indoctrinated for their posts. They subscribed to a general doctrine of "order" but were not motivated by any ideology which would instil fanatical devotion or nihilistic disregard of familiar legal and moral standards of conduct. Evidence of police brutality and of behavior not long customary in administrative practice is rarely to be found in the archival sources, except for the time of the coup d'état and the period of "extraordinary" administrative measures following it.

It may be concluded that both the theory and practice of political police from 1852 to 1870 show great continuity from the past. The Second Empire accentuated customary doctrines and techniques, but introduced few innovations. A function of general administration, political police flourished under a regime founded on increased centralization and a theory of government that legitimized a concentration of powers in the executive. Virtually unlimited in theory, police powers in practice were limited because attitudes, institutions, and social forces existing both in administration and in the general community put practical limitations on the omnipotence of the executive, the administration, and the political police. Theory provided ample bases for the police state; but practice kept the Second Empire far removed from the totalitarian models of the twentieth century.

L. C. B. SEAMAN (1911–   ) was trained at Cambridge University and is currently Senior History Master at the County Grammar School, Woking, Surrey, England. In a highly interesting book, suggestive of the writing of A. J. P. Taylor, Seaman has presented students of Napoleon III with a great number of novel interpretations. Among these is an upgrading of the importance of Napoleon III in Italian unification and the observation that "the contemptuous attitude usually taken towards Napoleon III's work for Italy is one of the shoddier bits of mythology of nineteenth century historians." Guérard called Seaman's book "an example of that rare honesty that demands clear cool courage." The author pursues the comparison of Louis Napoleon's career with Hitler's, using language blunter than Schapiro's but less intense than Namier's.*

Louis Napoleon:
Second Republic and Second Empire

One of the most interesting exercises in what might be termed comparative biography is to study the similarities and dissimilarities between Louis Napoleon and Adolf Hitler. In many respects their careers run on parallel lines and a study of either helps to illuminate one's understanding of the other. They rose to power in a remarkably similar defiance of the laws of probability. They performed the same function of first restoring and then destroying the power of the countries of their adoption, and each destroyed the international foundations on which the Europe of their time was built. In lesser things as in important ones, they are strangely alike. Both were strangers to the people they chose to lead. Hitler spoke German with an Austrian accent, Louis Napoleon French with a German accent. Each had his abortive putsch and consequent imprisonment. Strasbourg and Boulogne were to Louis Napoleon what the Munich Rising of 1923 was to Hitler. And if Landsberg meant much less to Hitler than Ham did to Louis Napoleon, *The Extinction of Pauperism* combined with the Memoirs of the first Napoleon bore much the same relation to the origins of the Second Empire as *Mein Kampf* did to the rise of the Third Reich. They were both essentially seedy characters and proclaimed it in their looks. Hitler's unkempt hair and his belted raincoat produced an inescapable effect of back-street vulgarity: and nothing can prevent Louis Napoleon from looking, in some of the less flattering photographs of him, like a shady Italian waiter recently dismissed from service in a fourth rate hotel....

Both had a gang. Both manœuvred into power with the connivance of politicians who under-estimated their abilities. Both sought to divert the gaze of the masses from politics by a concentration on material prosperity and by a calculated encouragement of public pageantry. The early propaganda of both reveals an adroit use of the device of stealing the slogans of the political forces of their day and pretending that they had found the secret of reconciling what the politicians had made irreconcilable. Thus, Hitler stole the Nationalist label from his dupes and the Socialist label from his enemies and persuaded both sides he was their ally. Louis Napoleon likewise offered France both "democracy" and "order," both social welfare and social discipline. He came promising universal suffrage to the masses, imperial glory to the army, Catholic liberties to the clericals, and an open field for profitable investment to the business man; just as Hitler simultaneously claimed to be liberating Germany from the monopolistic multiple stores while making it safe for the Ruhr industrialists. Finally one might observe that it was for not dissimilar reasons that the one built boulevards and railways and the other built autobahnen.

Yet there is an essential difference between Louis Napoleon and most other dictators and usurpers, Hitler included, which if clearly understood, provides the key to his character. Most men of this sort combine great ruthlessness with a daemonic possession. This was not true of Louis Napoleon. He had none of that fire in the belly that makes a man of action such as Napoleon I or Hitler, or even a Mussolini. He had neither drive nor organizing ability, nor the gift of steady application to routine administration such as characterized his uncle, or Frederick the Great, or Louis XIV; and his lack of the ability to come to a clear cut decision about anything is the most pronounced feature of his character. Whenever decision was at last grudgingly and uncertainly wrung from him he could only with difficulty be persuaded from going back on it. The *coup d'état;* the entry into the Crimean War and into the Italian War; the decision to take no action in 1866 and to take action in 1870, he regretted them all as soon as they were made, and endeavoured to go back on all of them, except for the decision of 1870, which proved fatal.

Louis Napoleon was a man whose tragedy it was to see a youthful dream come true.... Louis Napoleon obviously had more encouragement than most young men to dream such dreams, since he bore the Bonaparte name; but that name was his sole personal qualification for the practical business of politics and government. He inherited nothing whatever of the character of his imperial uncle; and scandal said that his mother could give good reasons for this.... Had he not been born in a Bonaparte household he would have found some modest niche somewhere—as a little-remembered princely publicist, a financially embarrassed dilettante man of the world, or as one of the more moderate deputies at the 1848 Frankfurt Assembly, a gathering exactly suited to his intellectual outlook and his limited ability.... He began as a political refugee and ended as one. The end was appropriate to the beginning; but in the high tide of his career he was acting hopelessly out of character. Few men have been more completely miscast than was Louis Napoleon when he posed upon the stage as Emperor of the French and the Napoleonic arbiter of Europe. It was a long time before anybody noticed how unsuited he was to his role, but that was because the other actors on the European stage at that time were inferior to him either in their intellectual ability or in the particular roles allotted to them. Cavour was a much abler performer, but his role was limited in significance and confined, so to speak, to the second act of the drama. Bismarck, naturally, claimed to have seen through the Emperor from the start, but Bismarck's conceit is notorious and the truth is that for all his ability, he did not dominate Europe until after the Second Empire was over.

Whether he was seeking power or exercising it, Louis Napoleon was irresolute, unmilitary, the reverse of ruthless, and devoid of that convincing air of authority with which some are born and which others acquire through the mere exercise of authority. Three examples will suffice. When it was a question of sending troops into the streets after the *coup d'état,* he panicked and left the job to Morny and Maupas. When Orsini's bomb claimed its victims outside the Opéra, Louis Napoleon wanted, like any decent private person, to go with them to make sure they were properly looked after. It was Eugénie who called him back to his official imperial duty, that of presenting himself calm and unruffled in his box in the theatre where the audience awaited him. When he advanced into Italy, the second of his name to do so, how different was the victor of Magenta and Solferino from the victor of Lodi and Rivoli. For the uncle it was the prelude to glory. For the nephew it was the prelude to a politically disastrous peace, made by a man whose visits to the scene of battle had turned him into a half-

fainting, half-vomiting mass of misery. That his personal linen was freely given to be torn into bandages reveals his humanity as a private person; that the official bandages did not reach Italy until the war was over reveals his incompetence as an Emperor.

It is thus erroneous to think of Louis Napoleon's seizure of power as the result of deliberate and careful long-term planning. What looked like the overthrow of a popular republic by a military despot, or even by a shady political adventurer, was something very different in reality. Neither the act nor the man in whose name it was undertaken can be understood unless the difference is appreciated.

In the first place, Louis Napoleon's election as President in 1848 was miracle enough for him to be very content with it. That it was three years before he assumed full power reflects not consummate patience but a consummate unwillingness to make up his mind.... Louis Napoleon would have been well satisfied with the Presidency save for two things. It did not provide him with enough money; and it was due to terminate in 1852. But until 1852 loomed in sight with still no sign that the Assembly would grant him either an increase of income or an extension of his tenure, he refused to budge. His only positive reason for delay was that if he had assumed sole power earlier he would have been dependent upon the army leader Changarnier, who in fact despised Louis Napoleon for not overthrowing the Republic in 1849 as he could have done without difficulty.

For their part, the politicians of the Assembly had their anxieties, too. Elections for a new President were due in 1852, and what might emerge from and during a renewed appeal to universal suffrage was a matter about which they were profoundly nervous. They had no candidate themselves, and the restoration of the monarchy had ceased to be practical politics. They had many good reasons for wanting to prolong Louis Napoleon's term of office and it is probable that if he had really tried he could have got a majority in the Assembly to vote for the necessary revision of the constitution. But he neither would nor could intrigue with the politicians, but only against them. Conspiracy was the only political technique with which he was familiar, and by 1851 it was clear also that a mere extension of his Presidential term would postpone but not solve the essential problem, that of how to stay in power permanently, and with an income adequate to his extravagant needs. Finally, there was the example of Napoleon I. Republic, Brumaire, Consulate, Empire—these were the stages in the first Napoleonic drama and the new Napoleon who was presenting himself in the title role of a revival of that drama had to fulfil the part prescribed for him by the historic text. Moreover, a lifetime of secret scheming with a few chosen outcasts like himself had fitted him to act in no other way.

Yet in a sense, although he manœuvred the politicians out of the seats of power, they may equally be regarded as having manœuvred him into the *coup d'état*. The members of the Assembly were too astute, and also too scared, to declare the abolition of the Second Republic themselves. They had killed it in June 1848, but there had been no death certificate and no public funeral, and so when in December 1851 Louis Napoleon brought out the body and gave it military burial he assumed at once the appearance of First Murderer. The accusation was to follow him all his life, and afterwards, to be elevated into an historical fact. By the *coup d'état*, Louis Napoleon did the Assembly's dirty work

for them; but thereafter they could always assert that their hands were clean and that they had been staunch defenders of the republican institutions that the bloody tyrant had destroyed. The politicians, too, were as afraid as was Louis Napoleon, of how Paris would react to a *coup d'état*. The attempt might fail; and they were determined not to look in the least like his accomplices. It was this desire to reinsure themselves against the failure of the *coup d'état* that led them to stage the somewhat comic efforts at official protest which were made on December 2nd. It would then be on record that they had protested, but had been silenced by the military (brutally, of course) and haled off to prison. Having thus done their duty they could in due course make their peace with the Tyrant and lend their assistance to the necessary task of giving France once again the benefits of Order.

The full effects of proceeding by *coup d'état* were made clear by the events of December 3rd. Whether the anti-Napoleonic demonstrations of that day were cunningly encouraged by Morny and Maupas or not, and whether the afternoon's firing by the troops was provoked by the hostility of the populace or was a mere display of force by an army under orders to terrorize the city at all costs, will doubtless continue to be a matter for dispute. What is inescapable is the fact that blood was shed at all on that day. It made nonsense for always of the Emperor's claim to base his power on the popular will. As was pointed out later on, celebrations and pageantry to commemorate the *coup d'état* were conspicuously absent from the organized junketings of the Second Empire. Napoleon III, least bloodthirsty of dictators, paid a heavy price for accepting the role of a Man of

Blood in December 1851.

For, in his career as Emperor, it is particularly important to see that the ways in which he was different from the dictators of the twentieth century are as remarkable as those in which he resembled them. His lack of ruthlessness was not the mere cowardice of a man with a weak stomach.... The evidence is clear enough that at heart he was a vague, well-meaning doctrinaire. If he was no Garibaldi, he was certainly no Cavour; indeed his ideas had more in common with those of Mazzini. This helps to explain the latter's rage at hearing Napoleon uttering theories about nationality, and interpreting the course of history, in phrases often extraordinarily like his own. It is also false to suppose that the Emperor had no policy save that of enjoying the creature comforts of his imperial position, much as he undoubtedly liked them. He suffered from having too many policies rather than too few, and from having policies which, like those of most of the left-wing doctrinaires of the nineteenth century, were inspiring on paper but vitiated by their imperfect and over-optimistic notions about human psychology. Napoleon III brimmed over with good intentions; to believe that he was nothing more than a sinister self-seeking adventurer is to fall victim to the polemics of his numerous enemies. Far too much so-called history about Napoleon III is based on the assumption that because he failed so catastrophically at the end he must therefore have been a very bad man and an exceptionally incompetent one. Yet in the breadth of his ideas, in the genuineness of his concern for Europe and the harmonious development of its peoples, he was a man of infinite generosity and good-will compared with the always cynical Bismarck and the often mean-spirited Cavour. They did not believe in

the causes they diverted to their own ends, whereas Napoleon did believe genuinely in Italian liberation and German nationality. One of the many mysteries of historical interpretation is the rarity with which it recognizes that Napoleon III alone made Italian freedom possible. Mixed as it was with other motives... his impulse to help the Italians was both sincere and exclusively personal to him. In all the evasions and equivocations and withdrawals that followed his meeting with Cavour at Plombières he was desperately trying to accommodate his personal wish to serve Italy to the interests and pressures against his plans which were operating both in France and the rest of Europe. In his dealings with Bismarck he was moved by a simultaneous belief in the progressive and efficient character of Prussian administration and in the greatness of the German contribution to European civilization, a factor about which Bismarck did not care anything at all. His feeble compensations policy after Sadowa was a concession to French hysteria and no part of a truly Napoleonic policy. In considering his policy towards Russia, also, it is important to distinguish the fundamental from the superficial. He was the first crowned head in Europe to desire the overthrow of the 1815 settlement (a fact which rarely secures him the sympathy of the many historians who disapprove of that settlement) and it was for this reason that he thought the power of Russia should be weakened; not as an end in itself, but as a prelude to the re-organization of Europe on the basis of nationality. That is why once Russia was weakened by the Crimean War he sought an alliance with her. No longer a menace, Russia could be persuaded to support or at any rate acquiesce in his schemes for European reconstruction, schemes which were far indeed from the idea of another Tilsit with which he was credited in London. His ministers thought Napoleon mad to prejudice his English alliance for the sake of an independent Roumania after 1856; but his support of the Roumanians is comprehensible if it is remembered that he really did believe in nationality.

As for Mexico, it is not without significance that Maximilian was as infatuated with the idea as Napoleon was. ... In opposing the Mexican clericals once he got to Mexico, Maximilian was, whether he knew it or not, behaving exactly as his thoughtful sponsor in the Tuileries would have done. The Mexican affair was foolish and showed a grotesque disregard for practical realities; but in its folly there was more good will than there was villainy or crafty calculation.

Finally, there is the circumstance that Napoleon III is unique among dictators in ending his career with a government that provided his country with more freedom than the government he started with. The visionary dream of a transient dictatorship for the good of the community to be followed by the abandonment of that dictatorship as the time of troubles recedes; this phantom that revolutionaries have theorized about and their opponents have derided as impracticable nonsense for over a century, Napoleon III almost succeeded in making a reality. It is much more a sign of his doctrinaire over-confidence than it is a sign of weakness that he Liberalized the Empire after 1860. He said at the outset that liberty would crown the imperial edifice; and the unusual spectacle of a political figure actually carrying out one of his promises has appeared so incredible that historians have been at infinite pains to explain the phenomenon out of existence. Yet to assert, for

example, that in 1860 Napoleon III's position either in France or in Europe was of such weakness that it compelled him to seek Liberal support is to assert what nobody believed. Men as astute as Cavour and Bismarck showed no sign whatever of regarding Napoleon III as played out. ...

What makes the attempt at a Liberal Empire so markedly doctrinaire, is first that it was impossible and second that it led to disaster. It was impossible for the Emperor to convince the Left of his sincerity because of the ineradicable memory of the *coup d'état*. In her extreme old age, Eugénie insisted that the *coup d'état* had been a mistake; for it erected a barrier of blood between the Emperor and the republican tradition that could not be ignored. And if, at the height of her influence, Eugénie was a bitter opponent of the idea of a Liberal Empire it was because she was so much more of a realist than her husband.

For to set up a Liberal Empire was to ignore even more vital facts in French political life. At the most critical period in the history of France and Europe, from 1867 to 1870, the freedom of the press and then the setting up of Parliamentary government, unleashed all that was most irresponsible and tawdry in France. For the politically vocal French had opposed the Emperor's timid efforts at army re-organization for purely political reasons, and yet at the same time used the "shame" of Sadowa as a stick with which to goad him into a war he did not want. Napoleon III himself saw no grounds for war in 1870 and did not want that war. It came about not because Napoleon III was then the effective ruler of France, but because in fulfilment of doctrinaire theory formulated twenty years before he had voluntarily ceased to be anything of the sort.

CHARLES H. POUTHAS (1886–   ) of the Sorbonne
is a highly esteemed authority on mid-nineteenth-
century France. In his course on the *Histoire Politique
du Second Empire* he argues (in an interesting contrast
to Aubry's analysis) that initiative nearly always came
from Napoleon III; he made policy and his
administrators were simply expediters of his ideas. The
following translation comes from another work, which
was published in Paris in 1941 when Hitler's power
extended over most of France. Do you find plausible
the linking of authoritarian government with economic
progress? From this account can you tell whether
Pouthas associates Napoleon III and Hitler?*

► *The Second Empire*

Between the *coup d'état* and the establishment of the new constitution, namely
from December 2, 1851, to the end of
March 1852, . . . Louis Napoleon's dictatorship rapidly dismanted the Second
Republic.

In a widespread purge, 218 representatives were arrested, of which the decree
of January 9 condemned five to deportation (only one, Miot, was actually de-
ported), exiled sixty-six (the *Montagnards*,
so-called "socialists"), and sentenced
eighteen to "temporary removal." Of
27,000 others arrested, the mixed departmental commissions, created on February 3 and consisting of the prefect, the
general, and the procurers, condemned

2804 to internment within France and
sentenced 15,045 to exile; 9530 to transportation to Algeria; and 239 to deportation to Guiana. . . . Of these sentences the
prince granted approximately 3500 reprieves or commutations.

Many institutions were substantially
modified: on December 4, freedom of the
press was suspended; on December 29,
the dispensation of beverages was subjected to authorization and inspection;
on January 11, the National Guard was
dissolved; and on March 25, all clubs
were suppressed once and for all. At the
same time the Prince broke with the
royalists. His decree of January 22
ordered the return to the government of

* Translated by Paul Morin and B.D. Gooch and reprinted from Charles Pouthas,
Democraties et Capitalisme (Paris, 1941), by permission of the Presses Universitaires de
France.

the Orleanist family estates which Louis-Philippe had granted to his children on the eve of his accession. The Orleanist princes were also denied the right to possess real estate in France. These reprisals gave the *coup d'état* a conservative and authoritarian aspect detrimental to its popular pretensions. But this is only the negative aspect of his dictatorship. The constructive activity of the dictatorship was considerable, and in contrast to the ineffectiveness with which the former legislative assembly is criticized, within a few weeks a series of decrees established a new regime inspired much more by the personal ideals of the prince than by the needs of the moment.

Few heads of state have prepared themselves by study and meditation as much and as long as Louis Napoleon, even before the long years of work at Ham. One can find in the *Idées Napoléoniennes* of 1839, and also in the *Extinction du Paupérisme* of 1844, the general lines of the system that he built upon the ground vacated by the monarchy and the republic, namely a *régime* that would be democratic but not republican, representative but not parliamentary, at the same time authoritarian and popular, as well as conservative and progressive. The essential idea, to be found in his official declarations as president, as well as in conversations and letters, seems to have been to turn the government and public life away from habits of political activity and to eliminate the occasions of parliamentary discussion and criticism. He would substitute for the "government of debaters" an efficient and practical *régime* that would promote social progress by the transformation of economic life, the amelioration of the plight of the working classes, and concern for morality: in short, by a kind of enlightened

despotism seeking its support directly in the consent of the people. The system corresponded to the character of the man, ambitious yet generous, authoritarian yet merciful, more flexible than the instruments of his actions but detesting the collision of face to face opposition. His solitary and cautious march toward supreme power had accustomed him to reflection and to taking deliberate decisions, while at the same time he was forced to cover his emotional and sensitive nature by an impenetrable mask. For eighteen years the lot of France was to depend upon the will and the vacillations of this man who was superior to the rest of his *entourage* and to the greater part of his opponents. The enormous number of approvals by plebiscite and by election indicated that the system, at least for some time, satisfied the desires of the majority of the country.

Following some fruitless committee deliberations, the constitution of January 14, 1852, was hastily drafted in a few hours along lines laid down in the proclamations of December 2. . . . It broke with principles that had inspired earlier constitutions, although the *Déclaration of 1789* was included under the first title as the basis of public law in France. . . . Abandoning the principle of the separation of powers, it organized the government under a president, elected for 10 years (renewable), who exercised his function through ministers, a council of state, and a legislative body. Thus there devolved upon the president powers larger than those which the executive usually had, notably the command of troops, the administration of justice (in his name), the right of reprieve, the oath of civil servants, and, finally, the right to initiate, to sanction, and to promulgate laws. This led to the disappearance of the ministerial prerogative of countersignature, of council, and of parliamentary responsibility as well as the subordination of those organs which exercised legislative authority "collectively" with the president, that is to say, the council of state, which became like the previous bureaucrats whose function it was to put into proper form the government's bills. The legislative body, elected for six years by universal suffrage, was reduced to discussing and voting upon laws with an illusory right of amend, but without contact with public opinion, since stenographic records of the discussions were forbidden and sessions could become secret upon the motion of five members. Finally the senate, nominated by the president, authorized the promulgation of laws that had been voted if these were not contrary to the constitution, to liberty and equality, to propriety, to morality, and to religion. In addition, by its recommendations the senate could fill gaps or propose changes in the constitution. These constitutional rights, even the supposedly fundamental notion of the responsibility of the president before the people, had in fact little substance except as regards the administrative organization of the government.

A few organic decrees completed the constitution. By decree of July 10, a high court of magistrates from the supreme court of appeals and of judges taken from the general councils was formed outside the political assemblies. A decree of February 2 established the procedure for electing the 261 deputies (one for every 35,000 constituents) and fixed in a loose fashion the conditions of age, the incompatibilities of public offices, parliamentary immunities, and the form of the ballot, cautiously withdrawing the right to vote in the case of seventeen indignities, including political misdemeanors,

and leaving up to the minister the apportionment of districts and the exclusion of the military. On the other hand, this hastily formed regime did not disguise authority: newspapers were regarded as essentially dangerous and responsible for all ills. The decree of January 17 codified all that previous governments had instituted to supervise and control them. ... In addition the government armed itself with the right to suspend newspapers for at least two months after two warnings and to close them after administrative or judicial suspension or in the interest of general security. The significance of all these measures is clear: the purpose was to turn citizens away from politics by leaving to the prince, who had been so delegated by the people, the care of administering the country. Henceforth "serious matters will be decided by mature deliberation."

All this was rapidly set in motion. A decree of January 25 named the forty members of the council of state, the essential machinery of the regime. These were men of competence and not selected for their political opinions, which, in fact, varied widely since this body included former members of the cabinet— of whom three had even protested against the *coup d'état*—representatives from the legislative assembly and some men whose fortune had in fact begun with that of the prince—such as Baroche, their president, and Rouher; Catholic monarchists such as Cornudet; and liberals such as Michel Chevalier or Quentin-Bauchart. On January 26 appeared the list of seventy-two senators, including former ministers, former deputies, former peers of France, generals, and magistrates such as Trolong, to which were added *de jure* the four cardinals and the eight marshals and admirals of France.

The elections were held on February

29 by that uninominal ballot which was to last until 1885. The government expressed its position in circulars to the prefects from Morny and then from Persigny. "When a man has made his fortune by work, industry, or agriculture, has ameliorated the lot of his workers, has made a noble use of his wealth, this man is preferable to that other who is usually called the man of politics," claimed the first circular. "What would not be the predicament of the French people without the intervention of the government?" claimed the second. It was important, obviously, that the government enlighten its electors on this point. "Since it is evidently the will of the people to finish what it has begun, the people must be put in a position to discern which are its friends and which are the enemies of the government that it has just established." Thus from the beginning was inaugurated the system of official candidacies. The results of this election could hardly be doubted. . . . Contrasted with 253 devoted partisans, an enlightened opposition was composed of four legitimists in the west and in the Herault; three republicans at Paris; Cavaignac and Carnot (on the second ballot), who did not however take their seats because of the oath; Hénon at Lyons; and a semirepublican at Lille, Pierre Legrand. The opening session took place on March 29 at the Tuileries, the chambers appearing at the residence of the president to symbolize the new balance of power.

Such were the institutions which lasted until 1860 without modifications except those brought on by the transformation of the decennial presidency into empire. This change was expected as inevitable. A circle of persons eager for places of power or reward were agitating for the empire, but the prince, who was more prudent, did not venture to commit himself before "A voyage of interrogation" in September and October of 1852—which he began, shrewdly, with those regions which had registered the more hostile reactions to the *coup d'état*, namely, the departments at the center of the valley of the Rhône. So triumphant were the receptions that the energies of the prefects were superfluous, and the prince was encouraged to discuss the prospect of the empire in his speech at Bordeaux on October 9 and allowed himself to be received as sovereign in Paris a week later. After a report of Trolong on November 7, the senate voted to reestablish imperial dignity and a plebescite on November 21 lent approval by a vote of 7,824,189 against 253,145. Curiously, however there were a considerable number of abstentions (2,062,798). . . .

The president detected a kind of sluggishness on the economic front and, to alleviate this, assumed for himself, in a senate decree of December 25, the right to modify tariffs and to undertake public works projects. . . . For the sake of good will, he annulled all current prohibitions against the press, pronounced individual amnesties for certain condemned political prisoners of 1848 and 1849, and, on December 9 authorized the return of all exiles upon the sole condition that they recognize the newly established regime.

Louis Napoleon had devoted only one year to running the course from consulate to empire. At the beginning of 1853, despite certain negotiations already begun in Sweden and in England, he decided to marry a Spaniard of high birth with whom he was in love, Eugenie de Montijo, Countess of Teba. The marriage occurred January 29 and 30, 1853. Thus all the elements of monarchy were now present.

The new system lived up to Louis

Napoleon's expectations. In a few months all political life disappeared. The double pressure of administrative and judicial policies plus a subtle enlargement of the area of forbidden subjects and the requirements for prior authorization eliminated most of the press.... Only the large Parisian papers survived: the *Constitutionnel,* the *Pays,* and *La Patrie,* all governmental organs; the *Univers* of Louis Veuillot, a Catholic publication; the Orleanist *Journal des Débats;* the legitimist publications *Gazette de France, l'Union,* and *l'Assemblée Nationale;* and finally two republican organs of moderate persuasion, the *Siècle* and the *Presse,* were saved by Prince Napoleon and tolerated because their polemics provided certain points of view (anticlerical mainly) on imperial policies. In the provinces, where the government exercised special scrutiny, there remained several advertising newspapers and, occasionally, a disguised legitimist or republican journal. All of these lasted only by dint of prudent effort and thanks to their skill in disguising criticism under allusions, witticism, or the detachment of theory. Critical private conversation in cafés and salons was overheard by an eavesdropping secret police that appeared everywhere. Only the *Institut,* the courts, and the ecclesiastical authorities escaped this repression.

Curiously, this society, which had enjoyed with passion all the fruits of liberty at the beginning of the Second Republic, now gave up its privileges without objection. Rural areas welcomed the empire enthusiastically. The working classes had broken with liberal politics after the June days. The bourgeoisie, except for intellectuals or prominent men who benefited in some manner from public life, sacrificed their right to criticize for the security of their interests....Government was never more mistress of the country than in those years of the empire. The administration took its officials in hand. The Oath of Allegiance weeded out those who were yet attached to liberal ideals. Harrassments of all types turned away the uncooperative.... Two public services that traditionally enjoyed a kind of independence were also subjected to the authority: the University ...and the bench....

Although not numerous—25,000 for 36,000,000 inhabitants—this corps of bureaucrats was a powerful instrument of authority because of the singular spirit that directed it, the uniformity of its activity, its obedience, the consideration that it enjoyed, and because of the general desire of a family that is rising to obtain "a place in the government." Over this provincial society there hovered the prestige and authority of the prefects. All projects of decentralization had been canceled and a decree of March 25, 1852, augmented their authority by giving them substantial powers heretofore reserved to the central government. They drew up local budgets, named subordinate officials, and could use the local police. The regulation of the press and of elections put all public expression under their supervision. The emperor had little to do to complete the work which he had begun as president. It sufficed for him to recall five prefects and to replace eighteen others. He increased their stature by a large salary enabling them to be the center of local society. They became the real guardians of the people ... who submitted completely.

All policies emanated from Paris. The personnel about the Emperor changed but little as time went by.... The council of ministers met twice weekly, but made no decisions since the emperor reserved these for himself in consultation with the chief of his cabinet, Mocquard, and signed all documents in audience before the chief of the relevant department. All of these were merely executive or technical consultants to a sovereign whose intentions were often unknown until the last minute but to whom they submitted with docility even though their own opinions had previously been opposed....

The business of government had thus taken on the form of an administrative routine: the drawing up of laws. Procedure was established from the first session in 1852. The legislative body was composed of newcomers, proprietors, businessmen, industrialists, people experienced in business, especially local business. However, it included neither bureaucrats nor politicians from former regimes except one, Montalembert, who was later to stigmatize the body in disparaging terms: "This cellar without air and light of day where I passed six years fighting with reptiles."... Considerable minorities appeared from time to time: 98 votes, for instance, upon the law of pensions in 1853; 51 votes in 1854 against the suits against Montalembert, and 39 on Fortoul's bill for the organization of the academies. The debates, however, were never political, but rather about the budget, the economy, or public works; and the procedures employed were calculated to drown out the opposition or to use it to modify proposed legislation. These bills, drawn up by the council of state, were studied in the seven agencies over which the deputies presided. Each department delegated representatives before a committee that decided any changes. Bills that were acceptable were carried to the council of state for ratification and next presented in public session for a vote as they stood. The committee, by its discussion and its

negotiations with the government, constituted the essential organ of the legislative process. One annual session of several weeks was not long enough for very much speech making. Further, ... the opposition was disarmed by the absence of stenographic records and general public indifference.

The regime, therefore, was the direct opposite of the pulsating life of the Second Republic, and even contrary to the evolution of France since 1815. But political concerns are not at the heart of the Second Empire. Its preoccupations are of a social and economic order. The birth of modern society is contemporary with the Second Empire; but, whereas in other countries such as England and Germany it emerged spontaneously and out of private initiative, in France Napoleon III was its deliberate initiator and guide. His economic and technical studies made at Ham and his visits to industrial centers in England gave him a taste and understanding of economic facts which make of him a modern man of bold outlook. Arriving with him in power, publicly and privately, besides men like Fould and Morny, the Saint-Simonians of business, were industrial leaders such as Michel Chevalier, Péreire, Talabot, Jullien, and Ferdinand de Lesseps. Vested interests, ingrained habits, or legalistic attitudes represented in the council of state and in the legislative body opposed the emperor's economic liberalism and spirit of adventure, forcing him to time prudently the stages of development, and compelling him to stop from time to time to let his ideas take root or to allow resistance to spend itself....

From the period of the dictatorship, a series of decrees had laid the foundations of the new edifice. First two essential facilities were created: transportation and credit. The system of national highways was already in existence and had only to be completed.... One billion francs were devoted to the secondary routes that fed the main arteries, and the influence of these roads began to transform the nature of village life. In addition, a network of railroads was created, whereas there had existed before hardly more than authorization and a general plan on paper. Great rail corporations were formed by the merger of fifteen small corporations.... In 1857 the major lines were constructed and joined to the German, Swiss, Italian, and Spanish systems. A new network of secondary lines was also added.... From 1900 kilometers in 1848 the collected lines in 1860 serviced 9625 kilometers.... Completion of the project entailed 7000 additional kilometers....

... The electric telegraph (open to the public in 1850 and for which there was created a special administration)... reached, between 1850 and 1857, Dover, Ajaccio, and Algiers, and transmitted 457,000 dispatches for France and 137,000 abroad.... Maritime companies were founded and subsidized by the state and developed specializations, both regarding ships and cargoes—the *Messageries Maritimes* in 1851, the *Compagnie Generale Transatlantique* in 1861. After a long investigation ordered in 1853, the law of 1857 organized five transatlantic lines, servicing North America, the Antilles, and the African coast, from Le Havre, Saint-Nazaire, and Bordeaux. The new merchant marine comprised 928,000 tons of sailing vessels (625,000 tons in 1848) and 84,000 tons of steam vessels (10,000 in 1848). Finally, in July and August of 1860 the government bought canals that had been privately owned.

This new transportation program presupposed an already existing system of credit superior and different from that of the *Haute Banque* existing under Louis-Philippe. The conservatism of this bank and its associations with the Orleanists compromised its relations with the emperor and his projects. The Rothschilds themselves were slow in being reconciled with Napoleon and put up obstacles to all his novel enterprises. In the field of finance the Second Empire was entirely creative. From this period date the great banks. The *Comptoir d'Escompte* was a temporary expedient at the beginning, but in January 1853 it became an independent bank whose branches were specialized banks for the major branches of industry; ... [T]he *Crédit Mobilier* of Péreire brothers and Fould (November 1852) was the most original innovation, designed—according to Saint-Simonian theory—to finance the national output by replenishing its own capital by issuing long-term stocks that served to offset the varying profits of industry, acquiring a revolving fund by short-term issues. Thus it furnished four billions for transportation, insurance, mining companies, and for public works, through the intermediary of the *Compagnie Immobilière de Paris* in 1858. The *Société générale de crédit industriel et commercial,* an international bank after May 1857, dealt in loans and discounts and served as intermediary for the transactions of the market. Other banks followed, namely, the *Crédit lyonnais* in 1863 and the *Société générale* in 1864.

The birth of these establishments of credit freed the Bank of France from the task of furnishing money to industry, a function which it was filling only with some reluctance. Considerable pressure from Napoleon had been necessary in 1852 to bring the bank to lower its rate to 3 percent....

Different, however, was the *Crédit Foncier,* founded by the government in

1852 ... to insure long-term mortgages, and, after July 1860, to insure loans to departments, communes, and public establishments. Their letters of credit were backed by low-rate debentures and premium bonds. The emperor had hoped to make the *Crédit Foncier* furnish credits to agriculture, but because of poor education in the rural areas, the system benefitted mainly the real estate men of the department of the Seine. ...

The treasury reserve, unused by Louis Philippe and still available after the crisis of 1848, was tapped by these new financial units and put at the disposal of the economy. Between 1852 and 1857 the new banks absorbed 4,700,-000,000 francs. The entire structure rested upon joint stock companies. ...

The model in these developments was Great Britain, whose liberal legislation the emperor never failed to praise. In addition he patterned his customs legislation on the British system. Between 1852 and 1856 he lowered some tariffs, notably in August 1853, the surtaxes on imports, and later the flexible rates on wheats and flours. On June 9, 1856, he submitted to the legislative committee a bill suppressing all tariffs, but was forced to withdraw it in the face of rising opposition from protectionist elements. At that juncture he resorted to diplomacy. On the basis of a memoir by the Péreire brothers and conversations begun with Cobden in October 1859, he secretly negotiated ... the commercial treaty of January 23, 1860, which suppressed all restrictions by adopting the system of *ad valorem* tariffs and of reciprocal lowering of tariffs. Similar agreements were negotiated in following years with other governments.

The result of this bold and liberal policy was translated, under the continual initiative of the government, into a flowering of all branches of the economy. Agriculture, however, experienced several difficulties due to poor harvests, especially in 1853, and to offset these the government further lowered tariffs, establishing in Paris a credit union for the baking industry in January 1854 and again in 1859. Léonce de Lavergne had noted earlier that "Half, and especially a quarter, of France, has an air of poverty which is painful to see." The government sought to popularize the discoveries of Boussingault, Dumas, and Liebig through courses in agricultural chemistry at Rouen, Bordeaux, and Nantes; by training agronomists at the institutes of Grignon, Grand-Jouan, and Montpellier; and by creating model farms and giving agricultural training in the normal schools. The laws of June 10, 1854, and July 13, 1858, encouraged clearing and drainage of lands and appropriated a hundred millions from the *Crédit Foncier* for loans for these purposes. ...

Industrial change can be measured by the fact that in 1850, 7147 machines in 7735 factories used 90,000 horsepower whereas in 1860, 12,357 machines in 11,696 factories used 153,000 horsepower. In heavy industries the great innovation was the change from wood to coke in smelting: in 1853, for the first time, coke outproduced wood by 60,000 tons; in 1860 coke yielded 580,000 tons against the 316,000 for wood. Coal production increased considerably ($4\frac{1}{2}$ million tons in 1850, $8\frac{1}{3}$ million in 1860) but the increase was nevertheless smaller than the demand (6 million to $14\frac{1}{4}$ million tons). The production of cast iron more than doubled from 400,000 tons in 1850 to 898,000 in 1860, while the output of steel similarly rose from 257,000 tons to 562,000 tons. These are indications not only of growth but also of technical change in industry. ...

In commercial relations, several changes were apparent: the birth, one might say, of extensive trade with South America and the countries of the Far East; the doubling of business relations with Germany, Belgium, Switzerland, and Italy; and an extraordinary development of trade with Algeria and with Great Britain.... Trade with Britain showed a profit balance. On the eve of the commercial treaty exports were double the imports and in the years following the treaty exports rose by 83 percent while the imports increased only 33 percent. Within France there was an increasing specialization of wholesale merchandising, each product well on the way to having its own distributors. The increase in the number of retail merchants is indicated by the size of the *Bottin,* which in 1863 had to be published in two volumes—Paris and the Provinces—and by the advent of the great department stores. The *Bon Marché* opened its doors in 1852, the *Louvre* in 1855, followed by *La Belle Jardinière* in 1856 and *Printemps* and *Samaritaine* in 1865 and 1869....

The transformation of Paris itself was a part of these great renovations. Soon after the *coup d'état* Napoleon had adopted a plan for major rebuilding that included the *Palais de l'industrie,* relieving the congestion in the Halles, completion of the Louvre, construction of the Boulevards Saint-Michel and Strasbourg, and the development of the Bois de Boulogne. On July 1, 1853, Haussmann, a new prefect from Bordeaux and the author of these projects, opened his offices at the Hotel de Ville. The law of May 2, 1855, gave priority to the renovation of the Hotel de Ville and that of May 1858 created twenty-one new streets and authorized the completion of the Boulevard Sébastopol and the Place de

l'Étoile. The installation of sewage facilities and expansion of the highway department served to increase the comfort and sanitation of the city.

The growth of the economy was to continue after 1860, but 1850–1860 was the germinal period.

The growing wealth of the country was indicated by a rise in wholesale prices, increased consumption,...and significant growth of savings and income. ...The value of inheritances rose from 1996 millions in 1848 to 2724 millions in 1860.... The development of insurance companies and of mutual funds shows a concern for future security normally associated with a surplus.... In 1852 the government considered taking over the insurance business and in 1857 the idea of making insurance obligatory, but opposition by the council of state caused these schemes to be abandoned and the insurance industry was thus left to develop freely....

This general increase of wealth led finally to a rise in population from 35,520,000 in 1848 to 36,510,000 in 1860. The acquisition of Nice and Savoy along with the normal increase raised the total in 1861 to 37,390,000....

The economic program, added to the expenses of war, was costly; but the country was easily able to carry the burden.... The years 1855 and 1858 showed a surplus in the budgets and the deficits of the other years were easily covered by treasury bonds. For the unusual expenses of war the emperor escaped the watchful eye of the banks addressing himself to the "universal suffrage of capital" by issuing loans for the first time directly to the public. This policy was astoundingly successful. The three loans for the Crimean War in 1854 and 1855 (for a total of 1,500,000,000 francs) were raised by an ever-increasing number of subscribers (317,000 for the third), while the loan of 500,000,000 francs of 1859 attracted 690,000 investors. The democratization of public finances was hailed, while the public debt had increased from 5560 millions in 1852 to 9401 in 1860, although the rate of interest remained constant. . . .

This economic transformation was bound to bring social consequences in its train. The structure of society was to be established along economic lines with classes coming to be defined more precisely upon the basis of money. While this process was merely getting started, former social stratification still remained and was even dominant. The agricultural class was the most important. . . . The industrial and commercial classes were growing but were as yet considerably smaller. . . . The geographic dispersion of industry was much the same as under the July Monarchy; but several important business concentrations were beginning to appear, in the vicinity of Marseilles and Lyons, in the Loire, the Haut-Rhin, in Normandy, and in the north.

This increased economic activity benefited the growing capitalism, but the workers' plight was aggravated by the uneven climb of prices and wages. . . . Another aspect of the new capitalism was the activity of speculators, the manipulators of money, who were denounced by moralists and attacked by the government. There were attempts to curb their activity in 1856 and 1857, but the proliferation of stock companies and the fluctuations of the market during this early period were irresistible. Scandals were common; the most far-reaching was the Mires case of 1860. All these testified to the new order.

Unlike prominent businessmen who profited from imperial policies, Napo-

leon pretended not to sacrifice to prosperity his concern for the moral and spiritual well-being of the people. In his speech of December 1, 1852, he gave as his goal "a stable government based upon religion, probity, justice, love of the suffering classes." All his public statements make an appeal for the amelioration of the lot of the laboring classes. Public aid given by the emperor and the empress from the privy purse exceeded 6,000,000 francs in certain years and included significant increases in educational facilities. . . . The drop in the crime rate is another sign of advances in education: 5000 condemned by trial and 219,000 before summary courts in 1850; 3500 and 154,000, respectively, in 1860.

For his constructive programs Napoleon looked to the Church and sought to enhance its influence on lay society. Government authority also found its proper role. However, a group about Napoleon III, namely Prince Napoleon, Persigny, Piétri, the Gallican jurists of the council of state and of the senate, defied ultramontanism and attempted to halt its progress. On occasion the emperor would rely upon these men to resist certain ecclesiastical pretentions, such as when he refused to abolish the organic articles or upheld, in 1853, the legal exclusiveness of civil marriage. . . . Yet he increased his paternalism, augmenting salaries and authorizing provincial councils. He linked the administration to religious ceremonies, allowed religious orders to increase, and entrusted to priests the university functions of teaching or of administration. In 1858, he made a trip to Brittany which ended with a pilgrimage to Sainte-Anne D'Auray. In pursuing this policy he gained some ascendancy over the lower clergy through Louis Veuillot and his increasingly influential *L'Univers,* a paper that was expanding under the apprehensive gaze of traditionalist bishops such as Msgr. Sibour, the archbishop of Paris, and Msgr. Dupanloup, the bishop of Orleans, and of liberal Catholics Montalembert and Falloux.

The clergy took advantage of the government's good will. The law of 1850 had established secondary colleges and grammar schools (which numbered more than 15,000 in 1860 with an enrollment of over 1,000,000 students) and also assured the establishment of an institution of higher learning, the *École des Carmes*. Restoration of the *Oratoire* in 1852 furnished the Church with its intellectuals. The Society of St. Vincent-de-Paul—whose founder, Ozanam, died in 1852—increased its obligations, providing visits to the poor, soup kitchens, patronage for students and apprentices, and libraries. Houses of charity increased. . . . In 1856 the funeral of Sister Rosalie, attended by the entire faubourg Saint-Marcel, showed how effective the clergy could be when supported by persons of prestige. . . . Thus after the horrors of revolution, the Church increased in strength among the middle classes while remaining strong among the peasants and workers.

Thus everywhere, in government, society, even in the activity of the clergy, there triumphed a preoccupation with economic and social matters. This was an unquestionable triumph for the regime, and political opposition became insignificant. Of the two royalist groups, the Orleanists were the most affected, since the coalition of the bourgeoisie and the clergy stripped them of their following; also the government was persecuting them in particular; . . . they were a staff without troops. The legitimists, who were more numerous and more powerful in the provinces, especially in Brittany, the Vendée and Anjou—and from time

to time supported by the higher clergy, such as Msgr. Pie of Poitiers—could have caused embarrassment by taking possession of local councils, but the Count de Chambord enunciated a policy of complete noninterference in 1852. Reconciliations between the two royalist branches were attempted in 1853 and again in 1856 but floundered on political issues. As a consequence, their opposition to the government was reduced to hopes and silent memories, black-listing imperial personnel, writing epigrams, or eulogizing parliamentary government at the Institute, as in the declamation of the Duc de Broglie at the French Academy on April 5, 1856.

The republican opposition was more potential than real. The exiles were a heterogeneous group, and the individual reprieves that Napoleon granted on frequent occasions, especially in 1856 at the birth of the Prince Imperial, robbed the republican cause of much of its drive. The Belgian government sought to avoid incidents with France and suppressed propaganda attacks in the public press. . . . The exiled were freer in England or in Switzerland, but attempts in London to organize, instead of unifying, provoked a schism of the two associations, namely the *Commune revolutionnaire* and the *Révolution*. Efforts by Mazzini, Ledru-Rollin, and Kossuth in 1865 to unify the various exile groups also failed. The role of the banished, therefore, was simply to maintain the republican myth.

At home, the "years of silence" deserved the title both from the inertia and disintegration of the political opposition as well as from energetic imperial policy. In Paris resistance was confined to polite conversations in the *salons* of Daniel Stern, Jules Simon, Goudchaux; courses by professors dismissed from the University such as Bersot, Vacherot,

Taine; conferences at the palace between young lawyers such as Jules Favre, Jules Ferry, and Floquet, following Crémieux, Marie, and other men of 1848; in a few studios of artists; in occasional funeral processions of some dignitary (Armand Marrast, Mme. Raspail, Arago in 1853; Lamennais in 1854; David d'Angers and Cavaignac in 1857). All this merely indicated that the ideal of 1848 continued but was not dangerous. In the provinces there was no opposition whatever.

Republicanism by this time had become only a doctrine. It was systematically expounded in works such as Proudhon's *De la justice dans la Révolution et l'Eglise* (1858), Vacherot's *La Démocratie* (1858), and Jules Simon's *La Liberté* (1859) and treated polemically by Thiers and Charras, later by Barny and Lanfrey. Edgar Quinet (1855) raised it to the level of a philosophy of history. Republicanism as an example appears in the memoirs of Daniel Stern, Louis Blanc, Lamartine, and Garnier-Pagès.... The regime countered with the exaltation of Napoleon I, the medal of St. Helena in 1857, and with the publication of *The Correspondance* starting in 1858. The republican doctrine was generally the same as in 1848, with one difference, its anticlericalism.... The republicans were not responsible for the sporadic efforts at direct action that took place: an attempted coup of two Belgians at Parenchies against the railroad upon which the emperor was due to pass in September 1854; an uprising of laborers at Trélazé August 26, 1855; attempts of Pianori against the emperor in April 1855; others by Bellamare in August 1855 and Tibaldi in July 1857; and finally on January 14, 1858, the bombing by Orsini. Orsini's plot was more serious by reason of its careful organization in London, the number of its victims (156,

of whom 8 died) and its consequences.

Republican weakness was revealed by the elections of June 21, 1857. With the exception of Montalembert, the government nominated the deputies whose names appeared as official candidates. The only danger seemed to be the possibility of too many abstentions. The selection of opposition candidates for the department of the Seine caused dissensions to erupt between the men of 1848— between the "doctrinaires," who wished only to attract supporters and not to participate in the caricature of a parliamentary regime, and the "young," who wanted action. In some wards there were two candidates: in others, none. Nevertheless, five republicans were elected in Paris: Carnot, Goudchaux, and Cavaignac, on the first ballot, then two "young" candidates, the lawyer Emile Ollivier, son of an exile, and the journalist Darimon, on the second ballot; at Lyons, Hénon was elected. The three "men of forty-eight" refused to take the oath and were replaced by Jules Favre and Ernest Picard. Thus was formed the group of "The Five." In Paris the opposition received the same number of votes as in 1852: 96,000. In the whole country it polled 665,000 against 5,500,000 for the official candidates. The indifference of the nation to this sterile political activity was manifested by two million abstentions. To avoid the embarrassment of duly-elected deputies refusing to take the oath, the Senate decreed, on February 17, 1858, that henceforth the oath be taken by the candidates before their election.

The attempt of Orsini was energetically followed by reprisals. The law of general security of February 19, 1858 (against which only twenty-four deputies voted), mixed administrative and judicial powers and armed the government with the arbitrary right to intern or to deport "for reason of grave evidence indicating them as dangerous" all political prisoners of the events of May and June 1848, June 1849, and December 1851, as well as all individuals guilty of a series of misdemeanors including all forms of active opposition. On February 7, 1853, General Espinasse, famous for his arrests of the parliamentarians at the time of the *coup d'état* and for his severity in 1852, was named minister of the interior and responsible for general security, replacing Billault: 400 persons, approximately, were arrested, of whom 300 were transported to Algeria. Finally, by March 25, the government announced in the *Moniteur* that the goal had been achieved. Espinasse left the ministry in June. After this repression the regime assumed again its former appearance, but the law remained in force as a warning.

All was forgotten, however, in the jubilation following the victories in Italy. The emperor even knew the joy of acclamation by the faubourg Saint-Antoine upon his departure and return from the campaign. Napoleon was confident enough of his position to be generous and by decree of August 15, 1859, he pronounced the amnesty of 1800 exiled, interned, or under surveillance. The annexation of Savoy and Nice, with the subsequent plebescites ... brought him the glory of erasing the traces of the second treaty of Paris. However, this year of 1860 was to see the birth, in the very bosom of the imperialist masses, of a double opposition: first, the lower clergy and the Catholics on the Roman question and, secondly, the opposition of the industrial protectionists following the treaty of commerce. But this was mere discontent rather than determined opposition and so far from being serious that the emperor generously conceded to the legislative body, by the decree of November 24, 1860, the right to deliberate and answer the Speech from the Throne, that is, the right to annual, open, political debate. Three ministers without portfolio were to be the spokesmen of the emperor.

Napoleon III could therefore say in 1860 that he had succeeded in the task that he had assumed. A genuine economic and social revolution was being translated into bursting prosperity and a general improvement of the living standards. The government presided over this in the most liberal and comprehensive manner; the country seemed to have forgotten its taste for politics and to prefer order to liberty.

With a pen which lends fascination to his subjects, PHILIP GUEDALLA (1889–1944) has written extensively on such historical topics as Palmerston and Wellington. In the selection below, Guedalla maintains that Louis Napoleon's destiny was merely to come to power and that, once in office, he had no guide for future policy or programs. A great minister could have saved him perhaps, but no such man appeared. While the liveliness and sparkle of Guedalla's style are appropriate to the outward appearances of the regime he is discussing, his main message is that the Second Empire woefully lacked originality and a sense of purpose, hardly an idea which Zeldin or Williams would find congenial.*

The Second Empire

Paris was an Imperial city once again, and the French army was the army of the Empire. It reentered the long tradition which had ended at Waterloo, and the trumpets which rang out in the dawn of the Second Empire were a faint, retarded echo of the trumpets of Austerlitz. The new government was in its beginnings a military government, and the army remained throughout the course of the Empire the most brilliant symbol of the iridescent transformation which France had undergone. In its jaunty reminiscence of the First Empire, its elegant protest against the dowdy age of Louis Philippe, in the swagger of its easy victories and the sudden downfall of its last defeat it expressed the whole temper and career of the Second Empire. ... It is the tragedy of Napoleon III, that he did not die until twenty years after his life had lost its purpose. He had lived, since he came of age, by the light of a single star which shone above the Tuileries and would make him, as he believed, Emperor of the French. The steady gleam of it, first seen above the hills in Switzerland, then dancing bright above Strasburg, faintly visible in the night sky over New York, then lighting a room in London, and shining through a barred window at Ham, had drawn him across the world to France. He followed it; and at forty-five, a pallid man with dull eyes, he was Emperor of the French and the husband of a beautiful woman. But the star flickered and failed, since on attaining his purpose he had lost it: it was the tragedy of an *arriviste* who arrived.

In his odd, silent way, behind the dull mask and the great moustache, the man had known he would be king. Since it was pre-ordained, his actions were unhurried, and he said always, *"Il ne faut rien brusquer."* He had seen a man follow his destiny out of exile, out of prison, to a predestined throne; and he was left with a queer faith in predestination. He had followed a star; and a King, a Republic, and seven millions of men had gone down before the inevitable event. But he knew nothing more of the future. It was written, and a wise man would watch the slow movement of events without thrusting rashly across the stream. His attitude was always that of a man who, in his own phrase, *"attend un événement."* "I never form distant plans," he once told a king's secretary, "I am governed by the exigencies of the moment." It was an odd confession; yet it was the wisdom of a man who had seen one thing happen inevitably and was left with a belief that all things were inevitable. The world thought him designing.... But he made few plans; he was indifferent in the choice of men to act for him, because he believed that without plans or men that which was written would come to pass; and when it came, he faced it quietly, saying as he had said to a Carlist prince, *"Quand le vin est tiré, il faut le boire."* So it was that for twenty years he seemed to drift, since it was useless to strive against the stream; a sphinx, since he answered no questions; an enigma to the world, since his own intentions were an enigma to himself.

He had been a man of one idea; and when it was accomplished, he was left without one. It was as though a man should climb a ridge of high hills and then have no direction for the great walk along the summits. Yet there was one principle which seemed to gleam vaguely through his opportunism. He still believed, as he had written in 1839, that the world should be made up of free nations, and he was haunted through his policy by a half-formed idea (had he not trained Italian guns against the *Papalini* in 1831?) that Italy must be freed by a Bonaparte. "Tell them," he had said to a woman in 1848, "that my name is Bonaparte, and that I feel the responsibilities which that name implies. Italy is dear to me, as dear almost as France, but my duties to France *passent avant tout.* I must watch for an opportunity. For the present I am controlled by the Assembly, which will not give me money and men for a war of sentiment, in which France has no direct immediate interest. But tell them that my feelings are now what they were in 1830, and repeat to them that my name is Bonaparte."...

In the grey dawn of the Second Empire, by the cold daybreak of 1852 the issues had been very plain. The broad alternatives of Empire and revolution had been sharply outlined in that clear light; and it seemed so easy to save society, so simple to strike enlightened international attitudes on the European stage. Slowly the day broadened, and under a mounting sun the Empire moved towards high noon. In the blaze of it there were French victories, an heir, a smiling Empress, and the world seemed waiting for Napoleon to remake it. But the day drew on, and in the milder light of afternoon the outlines blurred. The old certainties seemed to lose something of their sharpness and to fade, as doubts began to grow on the slow minds of France and Europe, and the paths of the Empire became less clear. The sun was still high, and the Emperor paced slowly in the sunlight. Yet it was past noon, and the shadows began to fall longer on the ground. There were deaths round the Emperor: Jerome, the old King of Westphalia, faded unimpressively out of life into the legend of the First Empire, and the Empress wore black for her sister, the Spanish duchess. There was a faint air of evening upon the Empire. Soon the light would fade, and it would be night.

It had been simple enough in the first movement of the Empire for a man not far past forty to govern France. Centralisation was the administrative tradition of Bonapartism, and a single will made all decisions. They were transmitted to the nation by the Imperial machine, and the functions of ministers rarely exceeded the limited duty of supervising its smooth running. Ability is not encouraged by absolutism of this order; his surroundings, as an observer wrote of them, were *"des outils et ... pas de compagnons,"* and since the Emperor needed no collaborators, he had found none. *"Le maître,"* as M. Mérimée saw him, *"n'admet pas trop, je le crains, qu'il y ait des hommes nécessaires."* But under the pressure of a later phase he began to be conscious of the need. His ministers had been little more than a procession of self-seeking mediocrities, each willing to subordinate his policy to the Emperor's, but all consolable for their subjection by the gratifying proximity of the public purse—M. Fould the banker, who drifted into statesmanship after a financial career that had been far, so very far, from exemplary; the grave Bar-

oche pocketing sinecures for his unpleasant son; M. Walewski, whose policy was so apt to vary with his investments; the hungry Haussmann, whose municipal finance inspired irreverent comments on the *Comptes fantastiques d'Haussmann;* and the simpler appetites of the smaller men. Their master had been indifferent in the choice of his servants since he disbelieved in the efficacy of human action to change the course of events and was content to rely, for such action as he took, upon himself. But as the scene darkened and the Emperor began to grope in the gathering gloom, he needed (and never found) a minister of the great tradition. There was no Louvet and no Colbert; and for ten years he was left muttering, as he had said almost fretfully to the Prince Consort at Osborne: *"Où trouver l'homme?"* ...

The experiment, which began in 1860, was an odd one. It was an attempt to govern France by the collaboration of men who did not believe in liberty with men who did not believe in the Empire; ....

Outside France the world lived in a succession of problems, to each of which the Emperor seemed anxious to apply a uniform solution consisting (it seemed ridiculous in 1860, but it was the wisdom of 1918) of a congress and the principle of nationality. The method had already been attempted in the case of Italy, where its success seemed only to be delayed by the illogical survival of the Papacy. The Emperor appeared to desire a repetition of the experiment when the Poles went out against their masters in 1863. There was a spate of Notes and despatches. But in a world which knew its lessons (and one could teach them as one sat smoking at the Tuileries) the

Polish question and the hovering problems of Rome, Greece, the Elbe Duchies, and the Danubian Principalities would all be quite simple, because all Italy would be Italian, Poland would be Polish, Germany would be German, and even in the Baltic the little kingdoms of the north would combine in a logical unit. It was so easy to reconstruct Europe with a blank map and a coloured pencil, and nothing but the obstinate pretence that the settlement of 1815 was immutable prevented the reconstruction. The imagination of Napoleon III was haunted by the malicious shadow of the Peace of Vienna. It had degraded his country, insulted his family, and cramped his project. He was a Bonaparte, and to revise it would be almost to reverse Waterloo. Twice at least, to the blushing Prince Albert in 1857 and to the less easily scandalised Lord Palmerston in 1863, he proposed a revision of the political structure of Europe. The proposal was even embodied in a general circular to the Powers. But the Prince was stiffly discouraging and "begged him," with a rare approach to gesticulation, "to open the book of history, which lay before him"; whilst Lord Palmerston, who although he was a Liberal rarely forgot that he was a landowner, felt that "those who hold their estates under a good title, now nearly half a century old, might not be particularly desirous of having it brought under discussion with all the alterations which good-natured neighbors might wish to suggest in their boundaries." The project was rendered still more ridiculous by a romantic design that the agenda of the conference should include the limitation of European armaments—*"des armements exagérés entretenus par de mutuelles défiances"*—and when it dropped, the Emperor was left alone with his large intentions. His policy was losing something of its old directness, and he seemed to stray among the diplomats with the lost air of a man of principle in a Peace Conference. His fiendish cunning (even Mr. Disraeli alarmed his old ladies with mysterious allusions to "the great Imperial Sphinx") was one of the tenderest illusions of a romantic age. . . .

The note of the later Empire (and in 1863 it began to swing slowly into the last phase) was uncertainty. New questions seemed to crowd upon it to which the simple catchwords of the *coup d'état* provided no answer. The Emperor was an aging man; the long moustache began to droop, and the hair hung raggedly above his ears. The mild manner was becoming touched with hesitancy, and when public business forced him to decisions, he fumbled a little with the problems of French policy. The slow drift of the Empire seemed to be floating him into a new world, among strange faces. But M. Mérimée, who had an eye for character, could see the truth: *"Le maître n'aime pas les visages nouveaux."* The old *personnel* was hastily adopted to the new problems; an old minister (it was the secret of Napoleon's failure to reconcile the Empire with democracy) was instructed to strike a new attitude; and his sovereign returned with obvious relief to the less exacting companionship of Julius Caesar. . . .

. . . In the spring days of 1866, when the Prussian artillery was buying horses and the Austrians were moving cavalry up into the northern provinces, both sides turned nervous eyes to Paris. The Emperor might throw an army into either scale, and he was the master of Italian policy. Prince Metternich, whose lady stood so well at Court, fluttered

round with offers from Vienna; and the
Prussian ambassador asked Napoleon to
name his price. He fumbled a little with
the maps (the Emperor was not well that
year) and muttered something about Belgium—or Luxemburg, perhaps—or was
there a town or so in the Saar basin?
It had been so simple to make one's
terms with Cavour in 1858. But somehow the world seemed more crowded
now; the provinces which one might
have asked for were full of Germans,
and it would be awkward for the high-
priest of nationalism to transgress the
sacred dogma of nationality. *"Ah! si vous
aviez une Savoie!"* said the Emperor a
little helplessly, and fell back into
silence. He made no terms with Prussia,
because (it was a strange confession for
an Emperor, and his country never forgave it) he was disinterested. He was
asked to approve the reconquest of Ven-
ice and the promotion of Prussia in
Germany; and since he approved already, there was no need to purchase
his approval. Besides, he might not win;
one must wait for the result; as always,
il ne faut rien brusquer. Napoleon was
ill that summer, and he had a sick man's
fear of sharp decisions. Anxious ambas-
sadors flitted in and out of his study;
but they saw little in his dull eyes beyond
the reflection of their own uncertainty.
... France seemed restive and the Emperor was far from well, "like a gambler," as Mr. Disraeli wrote "who has lost
half his fortune and restless to recover;
likely to make a *coup,* which may be
fatally final for himself." He made the
coup; but in those hot days of 1866 his
hand shook a little.

King William was riding through the
cheers in the Berlin streets, and Napoleon was huddled in pain, sipping his
water at Vichy, when the first demand
came to Bismarck. Mainz and the left
bank of the Rhine seemed a good deal
to ask for. . . . [A] calculated indiscretion
to a journalist informed the world of
the rebuff to France and alarmed good
Germans with the news that Napoleon
was waiting hungrily beyond the Rhine.
Napoleon was sick with dumb pain at
Vichy, and he seemed to turn blindly
like a weary bull as Bismarck planted
the *banderillas.* For a few days Imperial
policy was distracted by the sunlit tragedy of Mexico, as the Empress Charlotte
came to Paris for her audience and the
Emperor dragged back to meet her, sat
wearily through a bitter afternoon of
heat and railing, and watched the slow
drift of an Empire to disaster. . . .

It was the year 1867, and the brilliance
of the Empire (for it had still brilliance)
was a glow of evening, a vivid light upon
quiet hills that face a sinking sun. The
sky was still bright; but there was a
strange chill upon the Empire. The clear
dawn of 1852 seemed half a century
away, and quite suddenly the Emperor
had become an old man. Something in
Eugénie's sad-eyed beauty was beginning
to fade, and the Court had aged. . . .
Slowly the Emperor seemed to fade into
the background, to smoke his cigarettes
and speak low behind the great moustache in that far-away voice of his. . . .

It was an uncertain future, since the
old certainties of 1852 seemed to have
lost their hold upon the generation of
1867. The Empire had been made because France was haunted by the confused, ignoble vision of 1848. But the
men who had seen the great crowds go
roaring round the Hôtel de Ville and
heard the dreadful silence as Cavaignac's
infantry stormed the barricades were in
middle life now, and their sons could
remember little of the Empire except

the police, the censorship, and the heavy-handed *Préfets* who seemed to have re-made France in their own image, as M. Haussmann had remade Paris in his. The Revolution had been the *raison d'être* of the Empire; and in 1867 the Revolution was half forgotten.... The glamour of the Empire had begun to fade; it had not made a lucky throw since 1859: Rome was a riddle, Sadowa was a shame, and Mexico was a regret.... The faint dawn of 1870 broke over France with a pale gleam of hope, and the last winter of the Empire had almost an air of spring. New men, new names, new notions, seemed to come crowding on the scene, and the stiff outlines of autocracy were melting in the rebirth of the *Empire libéral* into the simpler, younger form of a modern monarchy. One could see, like shadows on the blind of a lighted room, the Emperor's tired, gracious gesture of surrender and M. Ollivier standing erect to take up, in the name of France, the burden of the Empire. And outside, in the sky above them, the dawn of 1870 was breaking.

The year opened in the pleasant stir of the new ministry. The decree which appointed it bore date January 2, and for a few months it lived a busy life of fresh endeavour. Someone had called it the *ministère des honnêtes gens*; and the old, faded figures of the Empire seemed to go back into their corners, as the band struck up an air of good intentions and M. Ollivier and his colleagues took their blameless way down the centre of the stage. M. Rouher was a retired grandee in the Senate; M. Haussmann faded inconspicuously out of public life; and even M. Thiers seemed satisfied. The Emperor played little games with the monkey which Eugénie had brought from Egypt or sat at Council with his back to the great fire, between M. Ollivier and the fierce moustache of General Leboeuf, drawing on his papers and making tentative suggestions. That winter there were great parties in Paris; Madame Ollivier wore the little dresses which made them call her *Sainte Mousseline* at the palace, and among the uniforms one saw queer, half-forgotten figures where M. Guizot came out once more to hear the talk and M. Odilon Barrot abounded with twenty years' accumulation of good advice. There was a strange, refreshing air of new beginnings, and the older men seemed to stand aside to watch the slow dawn of the *Empire Libéral*. But it was the dawn of a day that never came.

The following selection by ROGER WILLIAMS (1923–   ) of Antioch College has attracted considerable attention and by inference raises a host of questions about other interpretations of Napoleon III. A specialist in the Second Empire, Williams offers a number of provocative insights into the reign of Napoleon III. How would you relate his ideas to those of Pouthas? Does this selection, along with the earlier one by Payne, constitute an adequate answer to Schapiro? Consider this essay also in the light of Sencourt's comments; would you agree that in this context the article by Zeldin represents a sort of middle ground?*

Louis Napoleon: A Tragedy of Good Intentions

History is not just what we remember, but what we choose to remember. Accordingly, Louis-Napoleon Bonaparte may be accounted a failure, not only because his regime ended in defeat and disgrace, but because he has failed to attract the sympathy of historians, who do the world's remembering. At best loosely characterized as enigmatic, he has become the victim of an indifference which has been translated by most writers about him into terms of contempt.

Why has the Second Empire been regarded as so complete a failure? It is not enough to answer that it came to pieces in military disaster; other regimes have suffered similar catastrophes without, in addition, earning contempt. The truth is that Sedan has incurred more odium than Waterloo, not merely for military reasons, but because Louis-Napoleon's reign was less "glorious" than his uncle's, and his mistakes have therefore seemed the less excusable. What is worse, the errors of his lifetime have since been aggravated by identifying him with certain unsavoury systems and personalities of the twentieth century, and in particular with Mussolini and with Italian Fascism.

The reason why this comparison is inappropriate is not so much that it ignores important differences in the two

* From Roger L. Williams, "Louis Napoleon: A Tragedy of Good Intentions," *History Today*, IV, no. 4 (April 1954). By permission of *History Today* and the author.

regimes, as that it serves to obscure the singular character of the Second Empire, which owed much of its complexity to the nature of the Emperor himself. Granted that both the Second Empire and Fascist Italy emerged from similar social and economic crises, there remains no evidence that Mussolini consciously imitated Napoleon III's system of government. Both men had to meet egalitarian movements. . . . But there the parallel ends. Certainly, the middle class in France profited more from the neo-Napoleonic regime than the workers, but this is not a peculiarity of the Second Empire, since it is common to most French systems of government after 1789.

The various stages of the transition from autocracy to the Liberal Empire provide the key to the contrast between the Second Empire and modern fascist states. No one denies that by 1860 Napoleon III had managed to irritate most of the important political groups in France, but this is no proof that the Emperor began granting concessions out of fear of revolution. On the contrary, in 1860 he could point to a list of triumphs, which he had achieved in spite of opposition at home. The balance of power had been restored in the Eastern Mediterranean; he had contributed more than the Italians to their national unification and, in the process, acquired territories lost by France in the Vienna settlement; the Cobden-Chevalier Treaty of 1860 not only promised greater national prosperity but strengthened the entente with Britain. We need not be concerned here whether or not these achievements were all beneficial or likely to endure. It is more to the point that the Emperor saw in them the successful development of his programme.

In this connexion, a significant factor in the affairs of the Second Empire must be borne in mind. It is that fears, aspirations, and projects of those who surrounded the Emperor should not be taken too seriously. He was always solicitous of the opinions of others. . . . Yet, after hesitations, he invariably pursued the programme he had laid down before he ever achieved office. Invariably, too, he kept his plans secret from the opposition concerned until the project was either operative or the government too deeply committed to withdraw.

In short, any analysis of Second Empire policy must centre in the Emperor's own plans, and . . . contrary opinions, entrenched opposition, and the force of logic, acted only as a suspensive veto upon imperial decisions. This accounts for both the notable triumphs and the shocking fiascos of the reign.

The key to Louis-Napoleon is this: he was not only the heir but the victim of the Napoleonic Legend. Thus, his political philosophy is that of the eighteenth-century Enlightened Despots. . . . Napoleon I was the logical outcome of the teachings of the *philosophes*. Bonaparte was the supreme lawgiver who would legislate for stability and order, and therefore for liberty, since liberty was equated with order. In other words, Bonapartism was eighteenth-century Rationalism recast to allow for the effects of the French Revolution. When Bonapartism became a legend, later in the nineteenth century, it was in no way as a reflection of the actual events of the First Empire; instead, the First Empire was an unfortunately abortive attempt to organize liberty according to the best philosophic standards of the eighteenth century.

We may well doubt that Napoleon Bonaparte's intentions were in fact so idealistic as has been claimed, especially since he seems to have discovered his own selflessness only at St. Helena. But the point concerning us is that Louis-Napoleon never doubted the Napoleonic Legend. His mother, Hortense, saw to it that he was nourished upon the Legend from his birth. As a young man, he began to note down his developing political ideas, and these writings are throughout impregnated with the eighteenth-century concept that liberty is born out of order. Far more surely than his uncle, Louis-Napoleon was in the tradition of rulers such as Joseph II and Frederick II. When he finally achieved public office, Louis-Napoleon set out to enshrine the Napoleonic Legend in legislation. Small wonder, then, that Second Empire policies often lacked a sense of reality.

The Greeks would have seen in this career the elements of tragedy. From childhood the Emperor is committed to the enactment of an eighteenth-century doctrine, and strangely enough he comes closer to fitting the pattern of Enlightened Despotism than any of his eighteenth-century predecessors. With Order established, he moves forward to Liberty, but at this critical moment the audience sees that it has fallen to Napoleon's lot to play his enlightened part upon a stage where Bismarck is his antagonist. And so the final curtain descends with evil genius once again triumphant.

The eventual programme of the Second Empire was first drawn up by Louis-Napoleon in an array of pamphlets, collectively published as his *Works*. These *Works*... reveal how completely the man was a slave to the Legend, and they show how close was the relation between his early theory and his later practice. Accordingly, one must look at his theories.

Note, for example, this passage, which could easily be attributed to an eighteenth-century *philosophe:*

> "There can be no doubt that what is now wanted are immutable laws which shall insure the permanent well-being and liberty of the country.... It requires a strong hand to destroy the despotism of servitude through the agency of the despotism of liberty, and to save the country by the same means which otherwise would have subjected it."

Having read Montesquieu, Louis-Napoleon put forth a Bonapartist system of checks and balances. The executive power was to be vested in the Emperor, the legislature was to enjoy the deliberative power, and the powers of election and sanction were to belong to the people. Here, in 1832, we have a preview of the Constitution of 1852.... Louis-Napoleon has perhaps come nearest to engaging the sympathies of posterity through his belief in the principle of well-grouped nation states. Here again is to be seen the imprint of the Legend. He believed that Napoleon I had intended to bring about the revival of Italy. As for the German states, he says, "Southern Germany, emancipated from the yoke of the Germanic Empire, saw civilization advancing under the auspices of the *Code Napoléon.*" No student of the nineteenth century needs to be reminded that Louis-Napoleon obeyed the Legend in regard to Italy, but it is less well known that he favoured the creation of a Rhenish state. At least he did so until about 1866, when Prussian designs of aggrandisement were made plain, and the foreign policy inspired by the Legend began to collapse around him. Similarly, he felt predestined to do something for Polish independence—the precedent being the Grand Duchy of Warsaw created by his uncle—and this prevented the consummation of an understanding with Alexander II.

What was the Napoleonic goal to be

achieved by satisfying the various nationalist ambitions? The answer is liberty
and peace for all Europe. More than
once this theme is developed in Louis-
Napoleon's *Works*. He dreamt of an An-
glo-Franco-Russian entente, which would
regulate European affairs. This project
involved "completed nationalities and
satisfied general interests," a phrase
which the statesmen of the period pretended not to understand. But thus
Order would be produced, and out of it,
eventually, Liberty.

In short, Napoleon III's nationalism
was the nationalism of a good citzen
of Europe. It was the nationalism of
Herder and Mazzini, which identified
national self-determination with international peace, and it in no way resembled the Bismarckian nationalism of
Mussolini. The following quotation is
obviously not from Il Duce:

"We hear talk of eternal wars, of intermi-
nable struggles, and yet it would be an easy
matter for the sovereigns of the world to
consolidate an everlasting peace. Let them
consult the mutual relations and the habits
of the diverse nations amongst themselves;
let them grant the nationalities the institutions which they demand, and they will have
arrived at the secret of a true political balance. Then will all nations be brothers, and
they will embrace one another in the presence of tyranny dethroned, of a world re-
freshed and consoled, and of a contented
humanity."

Nor could these views on liberty be attributed to Louis-Napoleon:

"Men," said Mussolini, "are perhaps tired
of liberty. They have had enough of it....
Other watchwords exercise a much greater
fascination on the youth of today—order,
hierarchy, discipline.... The people do not
want liberty. They want railways, bridges,
drains, houses, roads, water, and light...."

By contrast, Louis-Napoleon wrote in
1832 that it was not so difficult to acquire
liberty as to preserve it. He wondered
how liberty could be preserved in an
age when those who ought to be defend-
ing it spent their time in incessantly at-
tacking it. His answer was that only a
Napoleonic régime could preserve liberty
by preventing both absolutism and a
Reign of Terror.

Louis Napoleon's *Works* are by no
means the only source from which may
be discovered his early ideals. Many
nineteenth-century radicals, who later
cursed Napoleon's name, had become
convinced in his young days that he was
a kindred spirit. Indeed, their bitter
denunciations of him after 1851 suggest
disillusionment rather than ideological
opposition. Shortly after the appearance
of the *Extinction of Pauperism* (1844),
Louis Blanc visited the author at Ham.
Though on several topics the two conspirators could not agree, Louis Blanc
genuinely felt that Louis-Napoleon's
ideas on social reform were little different from his own. . . .

In short, Louis-Napoleon embodied,
besides the political philosophy of the
eighteenth century, the industrial and
social philosophies of his own age. Once
this "Saint Simon on Horseback" came
to power, the various conflicting elements
in France found some facets of the Emperor pleasing and others repellent, according to their own respective interests.
The Saint-Simonians, who were never
Bonapartists, none the less gave their
support to Napoleon III. This famous
utopian cult believed that humanity
ought to organize all available resources
for the benefit of mankind as a whole.
To the Saint-Simonians the planned
economy that would put an end to the
exploitation of men implied authority,
not *laissez-faire,* and so they rallied to
Napoleon III. They lent their support
because he favoured public works, the
extension of public credit, and railway

construction. Some members of the cult, such as the Pereire brothers and Michel Chevalier, became important figures in Second Empire commerce and finance. Their faith in Napoleon was not misplaced, since he was always deeply concerned about plans for increasing production and improving means of distribution; and Chevalier's rôle in the consummation of the Treaty of 1860 is undeniable....

Historians have traditionally interpreted Napoleon III's programme as a series of manoeuvres designed to placate the various elements within France. Supposedly, his continuance in power depended upon his pleasing everybody. Thus, historians divorce the Emperor from his *Works,* and are apt to show him in the rôle of an opportunist, who wished for power and nothing more. If this were true, should he not have tightened the hold of his régime after 1860? For by no stretch of the imagination can the liberalizing of the Empire be construed to have meant greater personal power for the Emperor.

The argument may be put forward that Louis-Napoleon's *Works* were merely the propaganda of a political campaign, and that he did not really mean what he said. Yet, when in office, he took up and pursued so many of his early schemes that his *Works* cannot be so simply dismissed. His interest in Italy, Poland and Central America, in nationalities, international order and public works, his approval of Prussia's military system, and his solicitude for the poor, were evident in his *Works,* and, for better or for worse, moulded the policies of the Second Empire....

Why, then, should we doubt the Emperor's sincerity in 1859-60 when he moved toward his professed goal of a Liberal Empire? There were pressures upon him in 1860, but fundamentally they were the same pressures that had been extant from the beginning of his reign. The Crimean War, for example, which made Napoleon the arbiter of Europe, was forced upon a reluctant France, and the Italian war with Austria in 1859 was opposed by almost every French group—the Catholics, the businessmen, the farmers, and the superpatriots who regarded a united Italy as a threat to France....

Moreover, most of the Bonapartist advisers, with the exception of Morny, had been opposed to the liberal orientation in 1860, though by that date the Emperor had evidence that his programme was succeeding. The moment had come for him to "crown the edifice with liberty." This interpretation implies that the Emperor was impervious to criticism. Yet, how else is one to explain his blind devotion to a fixed set of principles? He was too kind not to listen to contrary advice; he merely disregarded it. His reign is remarkable in this respect, that he followed his own path, regardless of the forces that opposed him, and despite developments that should have dictated to him other policies. This tactic brought him his greatest triumphs and, also, in part, accounted for Sedan. In 1870 the ruler who had too often put Europe ahead of France found himself opposed by statesmen who put their own nation first. In foreign affairs at least, his gaze had been too much occupied with making the past fit the future, and he was cut down by those who were closer than he to the contemporary pulse. This is all the more remarkable when we remember that no one more than he was aware of the primary domestic problem of his age—the problem of liberty in the industrializing society....

The political amnesty of August 15th, 1859, forecast the evolution toward liberalism. This was followed by the famous decree of November 24th, 1860, which permitted parliamentary response to the speech from the throne. The political reforms that ensued in the next nine years were so far-reaching that later, in agony at Sedan, the Emperor of the French could only surrender his command and his own person; he could not speak for Paris.

History provides us in all epochs with numerous examples of dictatorship, but we must not suppose that everyone was a Fascist in the modern sense. Plebiscites, official candidates, censorship, and colonialism are not the whole story. The Second Empire began as eighteenth-century Enlightened Despotism; it ended with considerable liberty granted, and with a separation of powers that would have pleased Montesquieu.

And so one wonders if Napoleon III was actually so enigmatic as he is supposed. No one questions that his career was fascinating; his path was clearly outlined by the past, and his marked interest in history was evidence that he understood the reality of his own attachment to the past. It is ironical, therefore, that a man who undertook to write history according to the Napoleonic Legend should himself become the victim of a considerable body of historical writing which, to say the least, lacks objectivity.

In this article we have not sought to measure Louis-Napoleon's intelligence or political skill. His liberal and humanitarian interests have been our concern. And if his principles did not succeed, if his generous views were trampled upon by militant nationalism, does it belong to us to be contemptuous, or have we cause for regret?

A Fellow of Magdalen College at Oxford and a gifted
and prolific writer of diplomatic and political history,
A. J. P. TAYLOR (1906–   ) has produced works
that are pungently provocative and reflect careful study
and meditation. In the following essay he briefly
discusses many aspects of Napoleon III and comments
on much of the ambiguity regarding the emperor. In
the course of this he makes passing reference to the
views of many of the preceding writers. For Taylor,
Napoleon III remains a bundle of contradictions, but
in the end he was a man marked by December Second.
This Man of December was destined to become the
Man of Sedan. Could Williams or Zeldin have accepted
Taylor's conclusions?*

The Man of December

Some historical characters—I would
say most—become simpler as you know
more about them. The lines get stronger,
clearer; you see a whole man, you know
how he will behave, how he will face
difficulties, how he will respond to success. In the end he will go into one of
those two pigeon-holes that are so jeered
at and yet are essential for the moral
judgement that we finally have to make:
he can be docketed as "a good thing"—
or a bad one. But some few escape us and
baffle examination. The more we strip
off their disguises, the more new disguises
appear. Such was Louis Napoleon, the
man of mystery. Conspirator and statesman; dreamer and realist; despot and
democrat; maker of wars and man of

peace; creator and muddler; you can go
on indefinitely, until you begin to think
that he had no character at all, that at
the heart of him was a gigantic nothing.
All the greatest political observers of
the time tried to penetrate his secret:
Tocqueville, Marx, Thiers, Victor Hugo
—all failed to make sense of him. Bismarck called him a Sphinx, and added:
he was a Sphinx without a riddle. Was
it not rather that he had too many
riddles, and riddles to which he himself
did not know the answer?

Everything about him baffles inquiry.
Was he the son of his father? It seems
unlikely. Yet if not, then of whom? He
was a master of concealment. Whatever
his other failings, he left few traces. The

* Reprinted from A. J. P. Taylor, *Rumours of Wars* (London, 1952), by permission of
Hamish Hamilton, Inc.

letters of Napoleon I fill sixty-four volumes; the letters of Napoleon III, even if they could be brought together, would not fill one. He talked endlessly to a great variety of witnesses, but—like the smoke of the cigarettes that he was one of the first to favour—his talk was vague and intangible; it vanished into the air, leaving only a faint romantic odour, a thin cloud of mystery. He was a creature of the Romantic movement, a Byronic hero gone seedy and rather out-at-elbows. . . . The men who grew up in the thirty years after the battle of Waterloo played out their lives in the shadow of the great Napoleon, Napoleon I. He had done great things; they manufactured great phrases. When Napoleon I called himself Emperor of the French, this was an empire which stretched across Europe to the frontiers of Russia and Turkey. Napoleon III, as Emperor, ruled only over the old Kingdom of France, and all that he added to his empire in nearly twenty years was Savoy and a scrap of Indo-China. This was a typical gesture of the Romantic movement, and its great legacy to our own time: the name on the bottle was more important than the drink inside it. . . .

One writer has called Louis Napoleon "the modern Emperor"; another "the first mountebank dictator." Perhaps they are the same thing. The radicals of 1848 had claimed that they were bringing the masses into politics. The response had been disappointing. It was Louis Napoleon who first got the djinn out of the bottle. He said himself: "Other French governments have ruled with the support of perhaps one million of the educated masses; I have called in the other twenty-nine million." This determined his policy. Napoleon I did great things and then sought to present them in a strik-

ing way; Napoleon III looked for things that would appear striking and only then dressed them up as important. He deceived everyone, including himself. He could be an idealist free trader with Richard Cobden; a respectable sovereign with Queen Victoria; an unscrupulous schemer when he was with Bismarck. But there was also the myth that he had created for himself and which took in even him. He really saw himself as the all-wise dictator, the Cæsar who would reconcile all the classes in France and would remake the map of Europe. "When a man of my name is in power, he must do great things." He thrashed about like a lion in a cage, convinced that it ought to be ranging the jungle; always looking for great things to do, never finding them. He was no lion; he would have made an agreeable, though untrustworthy, domestic cat.

Great men in public life love power. That is what stamps them. They fight to get it and they use it ruthlessly when it is in their hands. Louis Napoleon would not pass this test of greatness. He loved conspiracy: the process of intrigue by which he moved towards power or the endless plans for using it. But he hated the action which threatened to follow these plans. For instance, the *coup d'état* of 2 December 1851 had been planned months before and put off at least twice. When it came to the point, Louis Napoleon hesitated again and might have put it off once more, had not the politicians of the assembly forced his hands, by beginning to make plans against him. And that, he thought, was unfair as well as being dangerous: like other conspirators, he claimed a monopoly in dishonesty.

The famous meeting at Plombières was a perfect example of his methods: the secret messages through somebody else's doctor; Cavour's trip to Plombières under a false name; the long discussions which left nothing on paper. The two men redrew the map of Italy in a few bold strokes; war and peace, and the future destinies of a nation, were settled between the puffs of a cigarette. Napoleon was roused only when they turned to discuss the trick with which they could provoke war; and conspirator's device was the thing that won his interest and held it for hour after hour. Cavour displayed all his gifts in devising schemes to lure Austria into the war that was to be her ruin; and Napoleon was delighted. It was very different when the time came to put the plans into action. Then Napoleon was all for delay, as fertile in excuses as he had once been in plans, and resentful when Cavour held him to his bargain. Six weeks before the war for the liberation of Italy broke out, he told Cavour that the war would have to be postponed for at least a year; and then no doubt he would have been for further delay. "You should know how to wait as I do." But his waiting had no purpose. He preferred to dream rather than to act; to make great plans, not to carry them out. He was a procrastinating adventurer; more of a scoundrel in his thoughts than in his deeds.

It was the same when Bismarck discussed the future of Germany with him at Biarritz in 1865. Napoleon supplied the keynote of the talks: "We must not make events; we must let them happen." Imagine a man who has lived by robbing banks saying: "We must not blow open the safe; we must wait for it to fall open." Bismarck is often credited with having tricked Napoleon at Biarritz: he got permission to go ahead with his plans for defeating Austria, yet promised Napoleon nothing in return. There was no trickery in this; it was what Napoleon wanted. But, again, not for the sophisticated reason so often given. He did not avoid formulating his demands for German territory for fear that Bismarck would think them too great and give up war against Austria. It was his old line of waiting. He did not know what to demand; he only knew how to wait, or so he thought. The conversations at Biarritz suited him even better than the bargain at Plombières. With Cavour he had had to commit himself to action, however grudgingly; with Bismarck he committed himself only to inaction, a course of policy which he meant to follow in any case. Bismarck was to provide the action; and Napoleon was somehow to profit from it. He was like a man who haunts the gambling-rooms in the belief that, if he encourages others to bet, he will one day draw a great prize.

The twenty years when Louis Napoleon ruled France were a period of great creative activity in every country of Europe. The steam engine and the railway spread across the Continent. In France, too, the Second Empire promised energy and creation; yet it was in these twenty years that France lost the leadership of Europe in politics, in economics, in culture. The Second Empire claimed to be Wagner and turned out to be Offenbach —a frivolous echo of the past, not an inspiration for the future. It was the bastard of the great Napoleon—in name, in policy, even in men. It was said at the time, that though Louis Napoleon was not the son of his father, everyone else at Court was the son of his mother. Morny was his illegitimate half-brother; Walewski the illegitimate son of Napoleon I. Its emotions were sham, also. This system which claimed to care for the masses was run by the most dishonest politicians who have ever governed France. All of them, even Napoleon himself, were convinced that the Empire would not last; and they plundered France while the opportunity lasted. Under the July monarchy Guizot had said to the French middle classes: "Get rich." The statesmen of the Second Empire applied this doctrine.

In foreign affairs there was the same contradiction between the phrases and the reality. Napoleon like to believe that his empire had sprung from the resentment which every Frenchman felt against the settlement of Europe made at Vienna in 1815 after the defeat of his uncle. In reality, this settlement had given France a position of primacy in Europe and had made her secure: if it was changed, France was bound to suffer. Hence Napoleon was constantly driven forward; and as constantly shrank from the results. In Sorel's words: "His name was his fortune and his undoing. His origins condemned him to success." Any other Frenchman might have defended the settlement of 1815; a Napoleon could not. Louis Napoleon believed that nationalism was the winning cause in Europe; and he meant to associate himself with its success. Despite his inaction, he could never support conservatism when it came to the point; and he tried to satisfy German and Italian nationalism without injuring France. In the outcome, he failed on both counts. He estranged Italy by holding on to Rome; he tried to make German unity stop at the Main; and by his very inaction took the decisive steps which ended the career of France as the Great Power of Europe.

Yet, with all his cunning, there was great good will. He really cared for Italy; he sympathized with Germany, or at any rate with German romanticism.

He dreamt always of a Europe in which there would be "a peaceful redress of grievances"; and he was the first European statesman in a responsible position to put forward plans for general disarmament. But, of course, they were plans in which the preponderance of France had to be recognized and made permanent. Disarmament, as always, seemed most attractive to the power that was on the decline.

Though he ruined France as a great power, he made France what she still is —as far as looks go. The Paris which tourists admire, the Paris of the opera and the great boulevards, is the creation of Napoleon III. Like every adventurer who has arrived Napoleon wanted something solid to show, something that would assert his permanence against the facts. And the Paris of Napoleon III has not done badly—better, at any rate, than the Berlin of Hitler or the Rome of Mussolini. Yet even this was a fraud. Its real purpose was to make long, wide streets so that a revolt could be put down easily, hardly a gesture of confidence towards the twenty-nine million. And having tricked others, Napoleon here misled himself. When his empire fell, there was no whiff of grapeshot; not a shot was fired. The boulevards had failed of their purpose.

We imagine nowadays—and even take pride in the thought—that dictators, swindling their way to power and keeping power by a succession of tricks, are a disease peculiar to the twentieth century. But there is nothing new in Hitler or Mussolini: Louis Napoleon had all their cards up his sleeve, except, perhaps, their brutality. He did not need a Nietzsche to put him beyond good and evil; he had arrived at the idea for himself. Certainly he owed his success to the same historic causes. The great French revolution destroyed the history of France before going on to destroy the history of Europe. Destroy tradition; destroy the political values on which a community has been built up, and only class war remains.

Marx did not discover this class war. He observed it in France and then generalized it as a formula for the future. That is the only way of the prophet: to foretell as the future what has already happened. Marx's prophecy has come off better than most, but in one vital point he went wrong. He supposed that the class war would be fought to a finish, that one side would win. And, since the bourgeoisie could not exterminate the proletariat, the proletariat would exterminate the bourgeoisie. There has been a different outcome: someone has slipped in between, played off one class against the other and exploited both. This, not his ragbag of ideas, was the great historical innovation of Louis Napoleon. He appealed to the fears of the middle classes when he made the *coup d'état* and presented himself as "the Guardian of Order." But he was also, in his muddled way, a socialist; he did more for the French working classes than any other French government before or since; and when he died a trade-union representative was the only man to come from France to his funeral.

But there was also another France, the France that had been created by the great revolution after what had been destroyed: the France that cared for liberty and the Rights of Man. This made the great difference between Louis Napoleon and his twentieth-century successors. The generals and civil servants and business men of Germany no doubt thought Hitler a barbarian; but once he had gained power, they licked his boots. The writers and political leaders of France never forgave Napoleon for the trickery and violence by which he had come to power. They turned their back on him and condemned him to rely on his fellow-gangsters. It is not surprising that many Frenchmen supported Napoleon, especially in his hour of success; what is surprising and honourable is that so many Frenchmen opposed him from beginning to end. It was easy to be against Napoleon when he turned out to be the man of Sedan. It was his doom that he was branded from the start, and branded in history, as the man of December.

Suggestions for Additional Reading

To probe further into the career of Napoleon III the reader might, first of all, explore fully those books from which a number of the present selections have been taken. Other pertinent works by authors appearing in this booklet might also be carefully explored, and they, in turn, will reveal a number of excellent bibliographies to point to still other works. There are two articles that might be particularly helpful: Alan B. Spitzer's "The Good Napoleon III," *French Historical Studies,* II, 3 (Spring 1952), pp. 308–329, surveys the face lifting that he feels recent authors have given to Napoleon III; and Robert Schnerb's "Napoleon III and the Second Empire," *Journal of Modern History,* VIII, 3 (September 1936), pp. 338–355, indicates the extent of historical scholarship on the man and the period as of the mid-thirties. There are other works not included in these articles or in the bibliographies referred to above, and there is a vast periodical literature on various phases of the Second Empire. The material in article form has only been partially incorporated into larger studies and continues to appear in a fairly steady volume. Though much of the writing on the Second Empire is in French, only the most basic and readily available are included in this essay.

Central to studies on the Second Empire are a number of classic works that have become models for other writers, either in terms of scope or general thesis. In this category is the magisterial *Histoire du Second Empire,* 7 vols. (12th ed.; Paris, 1912) by Pierre de la Gorce. Of equal importance is Emile Ollivier's *L'Empire libéral, études, récits, souvenirs,* 17 vols. and table (Paris,

120

1895–1915). An important republican interpretation may be found in Taxile Delord, *Histoire du Second Empire,* 6 vols. (Paris, 1868–1875). The socialist view of Napoleon III's reign appears in Albert Thomas, *Le Second Empire (1852–1870)* (vol. X in *Histoire Socialiste,* ed. by J. Jaurès, Paris, 1906); and Blanchard Jerrold has written the apologetic "official" family biography, *The Life of Napoleon III,* 4 vols. (London, 1874–1882).

Less massive but interesting and somewhat more objective are the following books: Edmund B. D'Auvergne, *Napoleon the Third, a biography* (London, 1929); T. A. B. Corley, *Democratic Despot. A Life of Napoleon III* (London, 1961); and Charles Seignobos, *La révolution de 1848; Le Second Empire, 1848–59 (Histoire de la France contemporaine,* VI; Paris, 1921).

Two recent works are particularly worth consulting. J. M. Thompson's *Louis Napoleon and the Second Empire* (New York, 1955) provides a somewhat different slant to Napoleon III, seeing him as a modern Hamlet. Another approach is that of G. P. Gooch in *The Second Empire* (London, 1960), which shows what Spitzer calls a "whiggish distaste for Bonapartist authoritarianism." Here the empire is presented through a series of biographical sketches and the procedure resembles Roger Williams, *Gaslight and Shadow* (New York, 1957). Much of this book by Gooch appeared piecemeal during 1957 and 1958 as articles in volumes 191–194 of the *Contemporary Review.*

A view that may be regarded as Orleanist is widely available in Jacques Bainville, *History of France* (New York, 1926). In chapter

20 Bainville discusses the Second Republic and Empire, noting that the Assembly that was overthrown by the *coup d'état* was a monarchist assembly and concludes, "If France had not had Napoleon III, she would have had a Henry V or a Louis Philippe II." Rather than strangling the republic as one would gather from Victor Hugo and other writers, actually "he was strangling a monarchy in the cradle."

Of special value are two books dealing with Bonapartism as a movement or legend: Albert Guérard, *Reflections on the Napoleonic Legend* (London, 1924); and H. A. L. Fisher, *Bonapartism* (Oxford, 1914).

There are many general histories of France which include careful considerations of Napoleon III. Among these are: André Maurois (pseud. for E. S. W. Herzog), *A History of France* (New York, 1957); Victor Duruy, *A Short History of France* (London, 1917); Denis W. Brogan, *The French Nation, from Napoleon to Pétain* (New York, 1957); Emile Bourgeois, *History of Modern France 1815–1913*, 2 vols. (Cambridge, 1919); and J. P. T. Bury, *France, 1814–1940* (Philadelphia, 1949).

An excellent survey of the Second Empire, presenting it in the general context of mid-nineteenth-century European developments, may be found in Robert C. Binkley's *Realism and Nationalism, 1852–1871* (New York, 1935). This volume has a thorough bibliography, which has been revised in the most recent printings to include works through 1958. A similar sort of presentation may also be found in the original *Cambridge Modern History*. In volume 11, *The Growth of Nationalities*, Albert Thomas has authored chapter 10, "Napoleon III and the Period of Personal Government (1852–9)" and chapter 17, "The Liberal Empire (1859–70)." The Second Empire figures prominently in many other chapters in the volume. In the *New Cambridge Modern History*, Paul Farmer discusses "The Second Empire in France" in chapter 17 of volume 10, *The Zenith of European Power 1830–1870*. As in the previous series, the Empire also appears in a number of related chapters.

Like Ollivier, many of the Empire's prom-inent people also left their memoirs or souvenirs. Most of these are in French but in English there is Viel Castel's *Memoirs of Count Horace de Viel Castel*, 2 vols. (2d ed.; London 1888) and the Baron d'Ambès (Heeckeren), *Intimate Memoirs of Napoleon III*, 2 vols. (Boston, 1912). Some interesting Orleanist views from the period can be read in Nassau W. Senior, *Conversations with M. Thiers, M. Guizot, and other Distinguished Persons during the Second Empire*, 2 vols. (London, 1878). Of value also is Sir William Fraser's *Napoleon III: My Recollections* (London, 1896) and Comte Fleury's *Memoirs of the Empress Eugénie*, 2 vols. (New York, 1920). The interestingly candid papers of Britain's Lord Cowley have appeared in two volumes edited by F. A. Wellesley, *The Paris Embassy during the Second Empire* (London, 1928) and *Secrets of the Second Empire* (London, 1929). They are also the main source for *Conversations with Napoleon III* (London, 1934,) edited by F. A. Wellesley and Robert Sencourt. Information on the emperor may also be found in the memoirs of the Earl of Malmesbury, James Howard Harris, *Memoirs of an Ex-Minister*, 2 vols. (London, 1884). Malmesbury was a long-time friend and intimate of Louis Napoleon. Other contemporary views may be found in works on or by other nineteenth century figures. The Second Empire figures prominently in many works by Victor Hugo and Karl Marx. Arthur W. Kinglake's *The Invasion of the Crimea*, 6 vols. (London, 1863–1880), in addition to covering the war, is of special importance in that in his chapter 14, in volume 1, he portrays Napoleon III as the great destroyer of democratic institutions. This is the origin of the extremely bitter anti-Napoleonic view which was the standard interpretation of Napoleon III to be found in textbooks for generations, indeed it is still to be encountered as some of the preceding selections amply indicate.

Most biographies, other than of the emperor himself, are in French. There is, however, Maristan Chapman's *Imperial Brother: The Life of the Duc de Morny* (New York, 1931). Regarding the empress, there is Augustin Filon's *Recollection of the Empress Eugénie* (New York, 1921); E. A. Rheinhard's *Napoleon and Eugénie: The tragicomedy of an Empire* (New York, 1931); and Erna Barschak's *The Innocent Empress* (New York, 1943). For another perspective, see Simone André Maurois, *Miss Howard and the Emperor* (New York, 1957).

Economic and social transitions during the Second Empire are treated in Arthur L. Dunham, *Anglo-French Treaty of Commerce of 1860 and the Progress of the Industrial Revolution in France* (Ann Arbor, 1930), and in Rondo Cameron, *France and the Economic Development of Europe, 1800–1914* (Princeton, 1961). The modernization of Paris may be explored in J. M. and Brian Chapman, *The Life and Times of Baron Haussmann* (Paris, 1932), and also in David H. Pinkney, *Napoleon III and the Rebuilding of Paris* (Princeton, 1958). Another aspect of life during the Second Empire may be found in D. G. Charlton, *Positivist Thought in France during the Second Empire* (Oxford, 1959).

Works on war, diplomacy and politics abound, particularly in French. In English there is Charles W. Hallberg, *Franz Joseph and Napoleon III, 1852–1864* (New York, 1955); Franklin C. Palm, *England and the Rise of Napoleon III* (Durham, N. C., 1948); Lynn M. Case, *French Opinion on War and Diplomacy during the Second Empire* (Philadelphia, 1954); B. D. Gooch, *The New Bonapartist Generals in the Crimean War* (The Hague, 1959); Robert H. Lord, *The Origins of the War of 1870* (Cambridge, Mass., 1924); and Michael Howard, *The Franco-Prussian War* (London, 1961).